PRAYERSCRIPTS

COMMAND YOUR Morning

30 DAYS OF PRAYERS AND DECLARATIONS TO
SEIZE YOUR DAY & SHAPE YOUR DESTINY

CYRIL OPOKU

Command Your Morning: 30 Days of Prayers and Declarations to Seize Your Day and Shape Your Destiny

© 2025 Cyril Opoku. *PrayerScripts*. All rights reserved.

No part of this publication may be reproduced, stored in a retrieval system, or transmitted in any form or by any means—electronic, mechanical, photocopy, recording, or otherwise—without the prior written permission of the publisher, except in the case of brief quotations used in reviews, articles, or devotionals.

Published by *Quest Publications*

ISBN: 978-1-988439-64-8

Cover design by *Quest Publications (questpublications@outlook.com)*

Unless otherwise indicated, all Scripture quotations are taken from the World English Bible (WEB), which is in the public domain. For more information, visit: www.worldenglish.bible

This book is a work of devotional encouragement. It is not intended to replace biblical study, pastoral counsel, or professional therapy.

Printed in the United States of America.

First Edition: July 2025

For more books like this, visit *PrayerScripts:* https://prayerscripts.org

Contents

Contents .... *iii*
Preface .... *x*
Introduction .... *xii*
How to Use This Book .... *xiii*

Day 1 1
   Awaken My Praise, O Lord 1
   I Command This Day 2
   No Weapon Will Prosper 3
   My Cup Overflows Today 4
   I Rise in Glory 5

Day 2 6
   Early Will I Seek You 6
   Ordered by the Lord 7
   Favor Is My Shield 8
   He Blesses My Bread 9
   I Am Yours, Lord 10

Day 3 11
   The Lord Has Given Me a Song 11
   My Steps Are Established 12
   Guarded by Angels, Kept by God 13
   Daily Loaded with Benefits 14
   I Arise and Shine 15

Day 4 16
   My Voice Rises Early 16
   Make My Path Straight 17
   You Go Before Me 18

    The Work of My Hands 19
    My Destiny Dawns Brightly 20

Day 5 21
    I Will Sing Through the Night 21
    Teach Me the Way 22
    A Wall of Fire Around Me 23
    Unfailing Mercy, Unending Supply 24
    Strength from Zion 25

Day 6 26
    Satisfied by Your Mercy 26
    Established in Righteous Peace 27
    My Mind is Stayed 28
    Rain of Blessing and Increase 29
    I Know Your Voice 30

Day 7 31
    My Worship Ascends Like Incense 31
    Doors Only You Can Open 32
    Strengthened by Inner Power 33
    Anointed for Overflow 34
    I Rise with Eagle Vision 35

Day 8 36
    This Day Is Divine 36
    I Rise Into Greater Light 37
    The Joy of the Lord Shields Me 38
    My Year Is Crowned 39
    I Stand in Your Presence 40

Day 9 41
- Let There Be Light 41
- Blessed in My Going 42
- Strong, Courageous, and Covered 43
- Planted and Prosperous 44
- I Am Called by Name 45

Day 10 46
- Joy Comes in the Morning 46
- Daily Bread, Divine Assignment 47
- Victory is Already Mine 48
- Goodness is Chasing Me 49
- My Light Breaks Forth 50

Day 11 51
- Awaken My Glory, Lord 51
- Show Me the Way 52
- Trained for Victory 53
- Heaven's Supply Is Mine 54
- I Am Made New 55

Day 12 56
- It Is Good to Praise You 56
- Guided by His Eye 57
- Dressed for Victory 58
- No Good Thing Withheld 59
- Let My Light Shine 60

Day 13 61
- I Rise Early to Seek You 61
- This Is the Way, Walk In It 62
- Mighty Through God 63

The Windows of Heaven Are Open 64
I Am Set Apart to Shine 65

Day 14 66
I Will Sing of Your Strength 66
Commit and Succeed 67
Greater Is He Within Me 68
The Power to Produce Wealth 69
I Live by Faith in the Son of God 70

Day 15 71
From Sunrise to Sunset 71
Establish the Work of My Hands 72
More Than a Conqueror 73
The Blessing That Adds No Sorrow 74
Led by the Spirit 75

Day 16 76
A Song in the Night 76
My Future Is in Your Hands 77
Trained for Battle, Covered in Grace 78
Abounding in Every Good Work 79
He Will Finish What He Started 80

Day 17 81
Come with Joyful Praise 81
Fully Pleasing and Fruitful 82
Fear Not, For I Am With You 83
Prosperity and Health for the Journey 84
Set Apart from the Start 85

Day 18 86
- Let My Words Bring You Joy 86
- Created to Do Good 87
- The Lord Is Faithful to Guard Me 88
- Bread for Today, Harvest for Tomorrow 89
- Wonderfully Made and Fully Known 90

Day 19 91
- I Wait with Worship 91
- I Commit and Advance 92
- My Refuge Is Near 93
- Delight and Be Supplied 94
- All I Do Glorifies You 95

Day 20 96
- Bless the Lord, O My Soul 96
- Light for My Path 97
- Surrounded by the Lord 98
- Giving Unlocks Overflow 99
- Being Transformed in Glory 100

Day 21 101
- I Will Bless You Always 101
- You Direct My Steps 102
- You Reach Down and Preserve Me 103
- Overflow in Every Area 104
- Seated with Christ in Authority 105

Day 22 106
- I Enter with Thanksgiving 106
- You Lead Me to Profit 107
- Everlasting Arms Hold Me 108

My Storehouses Overflow 109
Christ in Me, My Hope 110

Day 23 111
Light Has Come for Me 111
I Ask and Receive Wisdom 112
Surrounded by Angelic Defense 113
I Shall Not Lack 114
I Am Transformed and Aligned 115

Day 24 116
My Song Is My Weapon 116
Fruitful Because I'm Connected 117
Preserved from Every Evil 118
Beauty for My Ashes 119
I Will See God's Goodness 120

Day 25 121
I Will Bless You Daily 121
It's All Working for Good 122
The Lord Is My Safe Place 123
Reward Is Coming to Me 124
I Walk in the Light 125

Day 26 126
I Will Not Be Moved 126
He Leads Me Forward 127
You Are My Saving Strength 128
I Am Blessed to Bless 129
Filled With Hope and Power 130

DAY 27 131
- A New Song Arises 131
- Fully Equipped for Every Assignment 132
- Safe in Your Strong Tower 133
- Favor Follows Me Everywhere 134
- Walking Fully in the Light 135

DAY 28 136
- My Strength and My Song 136
- Guided by the Lord Continually 137
- Fearless in the Light 138
- Lifted and Supplied by God 139
- Anointed for This Assignment 140

DAY 29 141
- My Mouth Is Filled With Praise 141
- Preserved for Destiny 142
- Empowered to Overcome 143
- The Storehouse of Goodness 144
- Fully Equipped by Grace 145

DAY 30 146
- My Heart Trusts in You 146
- You Will Surely Do It 147
- I Trust the Name of God 148
- Increase Is My Portion 149
- You Light My Path 150

Epilogue *151*
Encourage Others with Your Story *152*
More from PrayerScripts *153*

Preface

For years, I began my days in a rush—my thoughts scattered, my soul unanchored, and my prayers reactive rather than prophetic. I knew God had called me to live with purpose and authority, but I often started my mornings already playing catch-up—mentally, emotionally, and spiritually.

Then I discovered the power of *commanding my morning*.

The idea wasn't new. Scripture is filled with examples of God's people rising early—not to scroll, worry, or react—but to declare, worship, listen, and rule. From Abraham to David, from Jesus to the early church, mornings were moments of divine alignment and kingdom release. And in this noisy world, we need that kind of spiritual clarity now more than ever.

Command Your Morning was birthed from that realization—and from my desire to help others start their days not with chaos, but with Christ at the center.

This 30-day journey was crafted with five powerful themes—**Praise, Purpose, Protection, Provision, and Position**—because I believe every morning must begin with honoring God, aligning with His will, declaring His covering, trusting His supply, and standing in our identity.

Each prayer and declaration is designed to be both deeply personal and prophetically sharp. They are not formulas—they are faith-charged starting points to awaken your spirit, renew your mind, and shape your day with God's Word.

My prayer is that this book becomes more than a devotional—it becomes a divine rhythm. A holy habit. A spiritual discipline that transforms how you wake, walk, and win in every area of your life.

May you never start another day without commanding it in faith.

In Christ's authority,
Cyril O.
Illinois, July 2025

Introduction

There is a battle over every morning—and every believer must choose to either drift into the day or *command it*.

Each new dawn is not just another page on the calendar. It is a divine opportunity. A spiritual threshold. A moment of fresh mercy and new momentum. How you begin your day determines how you walk through it, and how you walk through it shapes your destiny.

In the noise of this world, it's easy to lose focus, to react instead of rule. But Scripture reminds us that those who walk with God don't just survive the day—they govern it. Like watchmen on the wall, we are called to rise early, speak boldly, and align our hearts with heaven's agenda before the world has a chance to shape us.

Command Your Morning is a 30-day journey of prophetic prayers and powerful declarations crafted to help you seize your mornings with intentionality and spiritual authority. Each day draws from five themes—**Praise, Purpose, Protection, Provision, and Position**—anchoring your spirit in God's Word as you launch into your day.

Whether you're facing challenges, chasing dreams, or contending for promises, these prayers will help you silence fear, declare truth, and set divine order over your time, your thoughts, and your territory.

Don't just wake up—**rise up.**

It's time to command your morning—and shape your destiny.

How to Use This Book

Command Your Morning is more than a devotional—it's a daily spiritual discipline. It's designed to help you begin each morning with divine focus, intentional faith, and prophetic authority.

Each day contains five prayer segments, based on five foundational themes that align with God's promises for your life:

- **Praise** – Exalt the Lord and set your heart in worship.
- **Purpose** – Align with God's guidance and plans for your day.
- **Protection** – Declare His covering over your life and territory.
- **Provision** – Speak His abundance and sufficiency into every need.
- **Position** – Reaffirm your identity, authority, and destiny in Christ.

Every prayer is anchored in a specific Scripture. These are not generic prayers—they are prophetic, personalized declarations that help you speak God's Word over your life with boldness.

Here's how to use this book:

1. **Set aside time early each morning.** Before the world grabs your attention, give your day to God.
2. **Begin with the Praise segment.** Let thanksgiving lead the way.
3. **Read each Scripture reference.** Meditate on its truth before praying.
4. **Pray aloud.** Declare each prayer with faith and authority—this is spiritual warfare.

5. **Repeat as needed.** Some days you may pray through one or two themes. Other days, declare all five.

This is your time to rise in the Spirit, reject spiritual passivity, and command your morning before it commands you. Don't rush. Don't ritualize. Engage. Let these prayers guide your spirit into deeper communion and powerful activation.

Let this book be your companion for 30 days—and then a lifelong habit.

Your mornings will never be the same.

DAY 1

PRAISE

AWAKEN MY PRAISE, O LORD

> *A Song. A Psalm by David.* My heart is steadfast, God. I will sing and I will make music with my soul. Wake up, harp and lyre! I will wake up the dawn. I will give thanks to you, Yahweh, among the nations. I will sing praises to you among the peoples.
> —Psalms 108:1-3 WEB

Father, I rise this morning with a shout of praise on my lips. Like the psalmist, I say, "Awake, harp and lyre! I will awaken the dawn!" (Psalm 108:2). Let my worship be louder than worry, and my adoration rise before the sun itself. I will not enter this day in silence—I will command the morning with thanksgiving, declaring that You alone are worthy.

Every fiber of my being joins in praise—my voice, my hands, my mind, and my spirit. I refuse to let the rocks cry out in my place. I choose to magnify You before my schedule begins, before tasks and deadlines pull at my attention. You are my strength, my song, and my salvation. I offer this morning to You as an altar of praise.

Let the heavens hear my sound and let the earth respond in blessing. I don't praise You because life is perfect; I praise You because You are faithful. You are enthroned on my hallelujahs. Let my praise prepare the way for Your glory to manifest in my day.

In Jesus' name, Amen.

Purpose

I Command This Day

> "Have you commanded the morning in your days, and caused the dawn to know its place; that it might take hold of the ends of the earth, and shake the wicked out of it?
> —Job 38:12-13 WEB

Lord, I take spiritual authority over this day and declare: it shall align with heaven's purpose for my life. As it is written in Job 38:12, "Have you commanded the morning since your days began?"—yes, Lord, today I do just that. I speak divine order over my time, my thoughts, my actions, and my atmosphere.

I command chaos to bow to the peace of Christ. I call every assignment, appointment, and interaction to serve Your plan and bring You glory. I will not drift aimlessly; I walk in precision. My words are guided, my steps are directed, and my decisions are rooted in wisdom.

Let no minute be wasted. Let every opportunity be recognized. Today I live on purpose and with purpose. I cast off confusion and declare clarity. I cancel delay and speak acceleration. I embrace this day as a gift from You, and I take dominion over it in Your name.

I am aligned. I am focused. I am ready to walk boldly in Your will for my life today.

In Jesus' name, Amen.

PROTECTION

NO WEAPON WILL PROSPER

> "Behold, I have created the blacksmith who fans the coals into flame, and forges a weapon for his work; and I have created the destroyer to destroy. No weapon that is formed against you will prevail; and you will condemn every tongue that rises against you in judgment. This is the heritage of Yahweh's servants, and their righteousness is of me," says Yahweh.
> —Isaiah 54:16-17 WEB

Father, I step into this day covered by the power of Your Word: "No weapon formed against me shall prosper" (Isaiah 54:17). I declare this promise over my body, mind, family, and destiny. Every plot of the enemy is exposed, and every snare is broken. I take refuge under the shadow of Your wings and walk confidently in divine protection.

I decree that no conversation, decision, or attack formed in darkness will succeed against me today. I bind every word curse, cancel every demonic plan, and sever every spiritual entanglement that does not come from You. Angels are assigned to me. The blood of Jesus surrounds me. The name of the Lord is my shield.

I walk in boldness, not fear. I will not flinch, I will not flee—I will stand. The fire of God goes before me, and the presence of God surrounds me. I am untouchable by evil and unstoppable in purpose.

This day is guarded by heaven itself, and I am safe within it.

In Jesus' name, Amen.

PROVISION

MY CUP OVERFLOWS TODAY

> You prepare a table before me in the presence of my enemies. You anoint my head with oil. My cup runs over.
> —Psalms 23:5 WEB

Jehovah Jireh, my Provider, I thank You that today I walk in abundance. As Psalm 23:5 says, "You anoint my head with oil; my cup overflows." This morning I declare that lack will not define my day—Your provision will. You are the source of every need, and You never run dry.

I speak increase over my hands, peace over my thoughts, and favor over my path. You've prepared a table for me, even in the presence of resistance. I will not fear shortage or scarcity, for You daily load me with benefits. Doors are opening. Resources are flowing. Unexpected favor is locating me now.

Today I receive divine provision—not just for survival, but for generosity. My cup overflows so I may refresh others. I release anxiety about money, time, or strength, and I trust You fully. You are faithful to supply all my needs according to Your riches in glory.

Let this day overflow with evidence of Your goodness.

In Jesus' name, Amen.

POSITION

I RISE IN GLORY

> I said, "My strength has perished, along with my expectation from Yahweh." Remember my affliction and my misery, the wormwood and the bitterness. My soul still remembers them, and is bowed down within me. This I recall to my mind; therefore I have hope. It is because of Yahweh's loving kindnesses that we are not consumed, because his compassion doesn't fail. They are new every morning. Great is your faithfulness. "Yahweh is my portion," says my soul. "Therefore I will hope in him."
> —Lamentations 3:18-24 WEB

Abba Father, I thank You that I rise this morning not in my own strength but in the glory that comes from You. Your Word in Lamentations 3:23 says, "They are new every morning; great is Your faithfulness." Because of Your mercy, I stand renewed, redeemed, and repositioned today.

I take my place as a child of God—seated in heavenly places, clothed in righteousness, called by name. I reject every lie that says I am unworthy or defeated. I embrace the truth: I am chosen, accepted, and empowered by Your Spirit. I rise in authority. I walk in identity. I move in destiny.

Let no part of me shrink back today. I reflect Your light, carry Your Spirit, and speak with kingdom authority. The old is gone; the new has come. This morning, I step fully into who You say I am.

I don't just occupy space—I carry Your presence everywhere I go.

In Jesus' name, Amen.

DAY 2

PRAISE

EARLY WILL I SEEK YOU

A Psalm by David, when he was in the desert of Judah. God, you are my God. I will earnestly seek you. My soul thirsts for you. My flesh longs for you, in a dry and weary land, where there is no water…Because your loving kindness is better than life, my lips shall praise you. So I will bless you while I live. I will lift up my hands in your name.
—Psalms 63:1-4 WEB

Father, before the noise of the world begins, I rise to seek You. As David said in Psalm 63:1, "O God, You are my God; early will I seek You; my soul thirsts for You." This morning, I don't chase my to-do list—I chase Your presence. I hunger and thirst not just for results, but for relationship.

You are my portion, my satisfaction, and my source. The silence of the morning is sacred because it belongs to You. I tune my heart to Heaven's frequency and offer You the first fruit of my breath. My praise is not based on feelings—it's anchored in truth. You are good. You are faithful. You are near.

I set my heart on You above all else. As I begin this day, let my thoughts be filled with gratitude, and my lips overflow with thanksgiving. Let praise be the doorway that ushers in wisdom, joy, and divine encounters. Today, I will not wait for a miracle to praise You—I praise You because You are my miracle.

Early I rise. Early I worship. Early I command the atmosphere to bow to Your glory.

In Jesus' name, Amen.

PURPOSE

ORDERED BY THE LORD

> Let all things be done decently and in order.
> —1 Corinthians 14:40 WEB

Lord, I thank You that my day is not random or wasted—it is purposefully planned by Your hand. As Your Word declares in 1 Corinthians 14:40, "Let all things be done decently and in order." Today, I declare divine order over my mind, my schedule, my priorities, and my assignments.

Disorder has no place in my morning. Confusion has no voice in my decisions. I call my spirit, soul, and body into alignment with Your will. I break the power of procrastination, distraction, and delay. I am led by Your Spirit and focused on what matters most. I move with clarity and confidence.

I don't live by chance—I live by divine choreography. Every meeting, every encounter, every opportunity is guided by Your unseen hand. Let Your order replace my overwhelm. Let Your wisdom set the rhythm of my day. I refuse to be pulled in every direction—I walk the narrow path that leads to purpose.

Father, thank You for peace in the pace and meaning in the moment. Today, I live on purpose, with purpose, for Your purpose. In Jesus' name, Amen.

PROTECTION

FAVOR IS MY SHIELD

> But let all those who take refuge in you rejoice, Let them always shout for joy, because you defend them. Let them also who love your name be joyful in you. For you will bless the righteous. Yahweh, you will surround him with favor as with a shield.
> —Psalms 5:11-12 WEB

Father, I stand under divine covering today, and I decree that no plan of the enemy will succeed against me. As Psalm 5:12 declares, "For You, O Lord, will bless the righteous; with favor You will surround him as with a shield." I step into this day shielded by Your presence and favored by Your hand.

Let every scheme of darkness be overturned. Let every spiritual ambush be dismantled. I cancel premature death, confusion, and attack in the name of Jesus. No conversation, decision, or weapon formed in secret will prosper against me.

Instead, I am surrounded by favor. I walk into rooms where hearts are softened toward me. I receive unexpected kindness, divine appointments, and supernatural assistance. Your favor goes before me and guards behind me. I am not uncovered—I am carried in the care of the Almighty.

This morning, I place myself and my family under the blood of Jesus. Every step I take is shielded, every word I speak is protected, and every battle is already won.

In Jesus' name, Amen.

PROVISION

HE BLESSES MY BREAD

> You shall serve Yahweh your God, and he will bless your bread and your water, and I will take sickness away from among you.
> —Exodus 23:25 WEB

Jehovah Jireh, You are my faithful provider, and today I receive the promise of Exodus 23:25: "You shall serve the Lord your God, and He will bless your bread and your water." I rise today expecting blessing, not lack; abundance, not drought. I serve You with a joyful heart, and I know You are watching over my needs.

I release anxiety about finances, health, and open doors. You are not a man that You should lie—what You have blessed, no one can curse. Let the work of my hands be fruitful. Let divine multiplication touch everything I do today. I receive favor in my labor, honor in my assignments, and success in all I set out to do.

Father, bless my bread—every resource. Bless my water—every relationship, opportunity, and word I speak. I will not live in survival mode. I walk in overflow. Sickness is far from my house, and peace reigns within my gates.

Today, I expect the evidence of Your blessing. In Jesus' name, Amen.

POSITION

I AM YOURS, LORD

> Yahweh is my portion. I promised to obey your words.
> —Psalms 119:57 WEB

Father, I thank You for this sacred truth: "You are my portion, O Lord; I have said that I would keep Your words" (Psalm 119:57). I declare today that I do not belong to fear, failure, or my past—I belong to You. I am Yours, and You are mine.

I am not an orphan in the world—I am a child of the King. I walk through this day knowing that I am accepted, chosen, redeemed, and assigned. You are my portion, not just my provider. I do not chase what the world chases—I rest in what You have already given.

Let my identity in You silence every inner critic. Let my confidence be rooted in Your Word, not my performance. Let every step I take today reflect who I am: set apart, seated in heavenly places, and filled with purpose. I reject comparison. I refuse striving. I stand in the truth that I am called by name.

Today, I live from a place of rest, not rush—from identity, not insecurity.

In Jesus' name, Amen.

DAY 3

PRAISE

THE LORD HAS GIVEN ME A SONG

> The Lord Yahweh has given me the tongue of those who are taught, that I may know how to sustain with words him who is weary. He wakens morning by morning, he wakens my ear to hear as those who are taught. The Lord Yahweh has opened my ear, and I was not rebellious. I have not turned back.
> —Isaiah 50:4-5 WEB

Father, I thank You that this morning begins with a word from heaven. As Isaiah 50:4 declares, "The Lord God has given Me the tongue of the learned, that I should know how to speak a word in season..." I open my mouth in praise today because You have awakened me with purpose and placed a new song on my lips.

Before my feet hit the ground, I release worship into the atmosphere. My morning shall not be ruled by emotion or distraction—it shall be led by revelation. You've given me words of life, and I choose to use them to bless You. I declare that praise is my posture, and gratitude is my language.

Anoint my speech with grace today. Let every word I release carry healing, truth, and strength. Give me the discernment to speak what builds, not what breaks. My praise sets the tone for my speech, and my speech sets the tone for my day.

Today, I rise as one taught by the Lord—full of praise, full of truth, and full of Your Spirit. In Jesus' name, Amen.

Purpose

My Steps Are Established

> A man's goings are established by Yahweh. He delights in his way. Though he stumble, he shall not fall, for Yahweh holds him up with his hand.
> —Psalms 37:23-24 WEB

Father, I praise You that my steps today are not random. Psalm 37:23 says, "The steps of a good man are ordered by the Lord, and He delights in his way." I declare that my walk today is not based on guessing—it is guided by grace. I trust You to lead me on the right path, even when I don't know what's ahead.

I submit my plans to You. Redirect me if I drift. Correct me if I delay. Empower me to walk boldly where You are already waiting. I believe that You are orchestrating divine appointments, supernatural timing, and purpose-filled opportunities on my behalf.

I renounce confusion and hesitation. I step out with boldness, knowing You have gone before me. My life is not aimless; it is anchored in destiny. I am in the right place, at the right time, for the right reason—because You've ordered it so.

Today, let every step I take lead me deeper into Your will and closer to Your purpose for my life. In Jesus' name, Amen.

Protection

Guarded by Angels, Kept by God

> For he will put his angels in charge of you, to guard you in all your ways. They will bear you up in their hands, so that you won't dash your foot against a stone.
> —Psalms 91:11-12 WEB

Father, I thank You for divine protection that is active and powerful. As Psalm 91:11 promises, "He will give His angels charge over you, to keep you in all your ways." Today, I claim this promise for myself and my household. Angels are not just watching—they are warring on my behalf.

I declare that I walk under heavenly escort today. My going out and my coming in are covered. Accidents are averted. Evil is blocked. Darkness is exposed and defeated. I refuse to fear what surrounds me, because I'm surrounded by You.

I activate angelic protection over my travel, my body, my dwelling, and my assignments. No evil shall befall me, no plague shall come near my dwelling. I am not vulnerable—I am victorious. God is my shield, and His angels are my guard.

This morning, I take my stand under the banner of divine protection. I walk boldly, speak confidently, and live fearlessly—because heaven is fighting for me.

In Jesus' name, Amen.

PROVISION

DAILY LOADED WITH BENEFITS

> Blessed be the Lord, who daily bears our burdens, even the God who is our salvation. Selah. God is to us a God of deliverance. To Yahweh, the Lord, belongs escape from death.
> —Psalms 68:19-20 WEB

Gracious Father, I arise with thanksgiving, knowing that today is loaded with blessings from Your hand. As Psalm 68:19 declares, "Blessed be the Lord, who daily loads us with benefits, the God of our salvation!" I open my heart and hands to receive all You've prepared for me.

I don't live from empty to empty—I live from glory to glory, grace to grace. Every good and perfect gift comes from You, and I lack nothing in Your presence. I break agreement with fear of lack, poverty mindset, and striving. I receive Your provision with peace and praise.

Let every need be met today—spiritually, emotionally, financially, relationally. I expect favor to go before me. I expect doors to open. I expect You to bless what I touch and multiply what I offer. I'm not just surviving—I'm thriving because You are my Source.

Thank You for being the God who daily—not occasionally—blesses me with all I need and more.

In Jesus' name, Amen.

Position

1 Arise and Shine

> "Arise, shine; for your light has come, and Yahweh's glory has risen on you. For, behold, darkness will cover the earth, and thick darkness the peoples; but Yahweh will arise on you, and his glory shall be seen on you."
> —Isaiah 60:1-2 WEB

Lord, this morning I respond to Your call in Isaiah 60:1—"Arise, shine, for your light has come, and the glory of the Lord rises upon you." I don't shrink back. I don't stay low. I rise up in the identity You've given me and shine with the light You've placed within me.

I will not let darkness dictate my day. I carry the radiance of heaven. I am the salt of the earth, the light of the world, and a city set on a hill. I declare today that my identity in Christ outshines every label, every lie, and every limitation.

I stand tall in my calling. I reflect Your glory—not with pride, but with purpose. Your light has come, and it rests on me. Let Your presence be seen in my words, my attitude, my work, and my relationships. Let my life today be a beacon of hope and a mirror of Your love.

I will not hide. I will not dim down. I will rise and shine.

In Jesus' name, Amen.

DAY 4

PRAISE

MY VOICE RISES EARLY

> Yahweh, in the morning you shall hear my voice. In the morning I will lay my requests before you, and will watch expectantly.
> —Psalms 5:3 WEB

Father, this morning I lift my voice before anything else can speak into my day. As Psalm 5:3 declares, "In the morning, Lord, You hear my voice; in the morning I lay my requests before You and wait expectantly." Before I check a message, hear a headline, or make a move, I come to You first.

Let my voice rise like incense, and let my praise set the atmosphere for victory. I will not enter this day reactive or anxious—I enter in worship. I choose to fill the silence with surrender and the stillness with songs. I wait with holy expectation, knowing that when I speak to You, You respond with power.

I lay my heart bare before You. You hear me. You see me. You are already moving on my behalf. Let my worship become warfare and my prayers become prophecy. I declare this day is marked by answered petitions, divine interruptions, and supernatural joy.

Because You hear me, I will not fear.

In Jesus' name, Amen.

Purpose

Make My Path Straight

> Trust in Yahweh with all your heart, and don't lean on your own understanding. In all your ways acknowledge him, and he will make your paths straight.
> —Proverbs 3:5-6 WEB

Lord, I yield my plans to Your hands today. As Proverbs 3:5–6 commands, I trust in You with all my heart and lean not on my own understanding. In all my ways I acknowledge You, and I know You will make my paths straight.

I surrender every decision, every schedule, every next step. Where there is fog, bring clarity. Where there is uncertainty, release confirmation. I resist the urge to control what only You can direct. I believe that You are orchestrating every detail of my day to fulfill what You have ordained for me.

Let divine alignment be my portion. Let the crooked places be made straight. Give me discernment to recognize the doors You've opened, and the courage to walk through them. I will not drift—I will move with purpose and precision.

This day belongs to You. So do I.

In Jesus' name, Amen.

PROTECTION

You Go Before Me

Then I said to you, "Don't be terrified. Don't be afraid of them. Yahweh your God who goes before you, he will fight for you, according to all that he did for you in Egypt before your eyes, and in the wilderness, where you have seen how that Yahweh your God bore you, as a man does bear his son, in all the way that you went, until you came to this place."
—Deuteronomy 1:29-31 WEB

Mighty God, today I rest in the assurance of Deuteronomy 1:30—"The Lord your God, who goes before you, will Himself fight for you." I do not walk into this day alone or unarmed. You are already ahead of me, preparing victory in places I haven't yet stepped.

I silence fear and intimidation by standing on this truth: my battles are not mine—they are Yours. I will not be shaken by headlines, people, or unexpected pressures. The Lord of Hosts fights for me, and His presence surrounds me like a fortress.

Wherever I go, You've already gone. Whatever I face, You've already conquered. No ambush will surprise You. No enemy can overpower You. I declare this day secured, shielded, and saturated in divine defense.

My morning is guarded. My night is covered. My steps are protected.

In Jesus' name, Amen.

Provision

The Work of My Hands

> Let the favor of the Lord our God be on us; establish the work of our hands for us; yes, establish the work of our hands.
> —Psalms 90:17 WEB

Father, I thank You for being the One who blesses not just what I need—but what I do. As Psalm 90:17 says, "May the favor of the Lord our God rest on us; establish the work of our hands for us—yes, establish the work of our hands."

Today I ask You to breathe on everything I touch. Let Your favor rest on my labor, my ideas, my conversations, and my assignments. Prosper what is holy. Multiply what is excellent. Establish what carries eternal value.

I rebuke weariness and futility. I will not work in vain. I will not strive without fruit. You bless not just my income, but my impact. Let this day bring forth visible evidence of Your favor. Let doors open where there were none. Let what seemed impossible yesterday be accomplished today.

Your blessing makes me rich in results, not just resources.

In Jesus' name, Amen.

Position

My Destiny Dawns Brightly

> Life shall be clearer than the noonday. Though there is darkness, it shall be as the morning. You shall be secure, because there is hope. Yes, you shall search, and shall take your rest in safety. Also you shall lie down, and no one shall make you afraid. Yes, many shall court your favor.
> —Job 11:17-19 WEB

I decree that my daybreak is radiant with purpose and power. My path grows brighter with each step, and I will not dwell in yesterday's shadows. I am positioned for destiny, and the light of God illuminates my way.

Every dark place is scattered by Your truth. I will no longer be held hostage by confusion, regret, or fear. My eyes are fixed forward, and I am stepping into new levels of clarity and confidence. The rising light signals new beginnings and fresh favor.

Thank You, Lord, for redeeming my time and realigning my focus. I will not miss my moment. I rise today with renewed strength, prepared to walk fully in who You've called me to be.

In Jesus' name, Amen.

DAY 5

PRAISE

I WILL SING THROUGH THE NIGHT

> Cause me to hear your loving kindness in the morning, for I trust in you. Cause me to know the way in which I should walk, for I lift up my soul to you.
> —Psalms 143:8 WEB

Father, Your love endures beyond sunrise and Your faithfulness reaches into the night. As Psalm 143:8 declares, "Let the morning bring me word of Your unfailing love, for I have put my trust in You." Before the day unfolds, I choose to sing of Your goodness and declare that Your love surrounds me like the morning light.

You are not only the God of my morning—you are the God of my moments. I lift my voice in praise not because everything is perfect, but because You are. You've never failed me. You've never left me. You've never stopped loving me. My trust is rooted in who You are, not what I feel.

Today, let my praise break chains. Let my gratitude shift atmospheres. Let my worship open heaven over this day. I don't need to see results to give You glory—I give You glory because You reign.

I release every burden into Your hands, and I lift every praise with my mouth. In Jesus' name, Amen.

Purpose

Teach Me the Way

> Show me your ways, Yahweh. Teach me your paths. Guide me in your truth, and teach me, For you are the God of my salvation, I wait for you all day long.
> —Psalms 25:4-5 WEB

Lord, this morning I echo the heart of the psalmist in Psalm 25:4–5: "Show me Your ways, Lord, teach me Your paths. Guide me in Your truth and teach me, for You are God my Savior, and my hope is in You all day long." I don't want to rush into this day with my own understanding—I want to be taught by You.

I humble myself before Your wisdom. Lead me away from detours, delays, and distractions. Reveal what is real. Expose what is counterfeit. Teach me how to walk in the rhythm of grace, not the pressure of performance.

Guide my heart, my words, and my decisions. Let nothing be done out of impulse, fear, or striving. I ask You to lead me step-by-step, even if all I see is the next one. Your path is perfect. Your truth is life. And Your leadership never fails.

My hope is not in outcomes—it's in Your voice.

In Jesus' name, Amen.

PROTECTION

A Wall of Fire Around Me

> And said to him, "Run, speak to this young man, saying, 'Jerusalem will be inhabited as villages without walls, because of the multitude of men and livestock in it. For I,' says Yahweh, 'will be to her a wall of fire around it, and I will be the glory in the middle of her.
> —Zechariah 2:4-5 WEB

Holy Defender, today I receive the promise of Zechariah 2:5: "'And I myself will be a wall of fire around it,' declares the Lord, 'and I will be its glory within.'" I thank You that I don't need to build my own defenses—You are my covering, my fire, my fortress.

Let every plan of the enemy be consumed. Let every trap be exposed. I declare that this day is surrounded by the fire of Your presence. No evil shall enter. No curse shall land. No fear shall find footing.

I belong to You, and You fiercely protect what's Yours. My mind is shielded, my family is guarded, and my destiny is untouchable. I'm not just protected from harm—I'm saturated in glory. You are not just keeping me safe; You are showing Yourself strong.

I walk boldly into this day surrounded by holy fire.

In Jesus' name, Amen.

Provision

Unfailing Mercy, Unending Supply

> Many sorrows come to the wicked, but loving kindness shall surround him who trusts in Yahweh.
> —Psalms 32:10 WEB

Gracious Father, I thank You for the mercy that meets me every morning. As Psalm 32:10 declares, "Many are the woes of the wicked, but the Lord's unfailing love surrounds the one who trusts in Him." I declare that I am surrounded—not by lack, but by love; not by shortage, but by supply.

I trust You with every need. I place every concern into Your hands. I cancel every agreement with fear, anxiety, and limitation. I declare that unexpected provision will locate me. Favor will meet me. Doors will open for me. You withhold no good thing from those who walk uprightly.

Let Your love surround my work, my finances, my relationships, and my daily needs. Because I trust in You, I expect to be blessed. I expect to be favored. I expect to walk in more than enough.

Today, I live under the banner of Your unfailing provision.

In Jesus' name, Amen.

POSITION

STRENGTH FROM ZION

For the Chief Musician. A Psalm by David. May Yahweh answer you in the day of trouble. May the name of the God of Jacob set you up on high, send you help from the sanctuary, grant you support from Zion, remember all your offerings, and accept your burned sacrifice. Selah.
—Psalms 20:1-3 WEB

Father, I receive strength from Your presence today. As Psalm 20:2 declares, "May He send you help from the sanctuary and grant you support from Zion." I don't rely on my own strength—I rely on heaven's supply.

I take my position as a child of God, seated with Christ, empowered by grace, and clothed in righteousness. I don't beg for help—I walk in it. I don't crawl through this day—I rise into it with authority. I am not an afterthought—I am chosen, equipped, and backed by heaven.

Let strength arise where I feel weak. Let identity override insecurity. Let divine backing silence every enemy. I am not alone. I am not unarmed. I am not uncertain. I know who I am, and I know who walks with me.

Today, I move with confidence and kingdom authority—because I am positioned in Christ.

In Jesus' name, Amen.

DAY 6

PRAISE

SATISFIED BY YOUR MERCY

> Satisfy us in the morning with your loving kindness, that we may rejoice and be glad all our days. Make us glad for as many days as you have afflicted us, for as many years as we have seen evil.
> —Psalms 90:14-15 WEB

I declare that this morning, my soul is fully satisfied in You, O Lord. I rise not in complaint or confusion but in deep gratitude for Your unfailing love. You have met me again with mercy, and that mercy is more than enough. From the moment my eyes opened, I was embraced by Your compassion, and I choose to rejoice in it all day long.

Let every part of my being—my thoughts, my voice, my actions—echo back praise to the One who daily satisfies me. I will not be consumed by the burdens of yesterday or the unknowns of tomorrow. Instead, I lift my eyes to the hills, knowing my help and my joy come from You. You are my morning portion and my evening peace.

Thank You for the kind of love that doesn't expire. Your mercy refreshes me, renews me, and restores my hope. No matter what unfolds today, I will rejoice because I am loved, kept, and known by You. This day is filled with songs of joy because You have filled me with Yourself.

In Jesus' name, Amen.

Purpose

Established in Righteous Peace

> In righteousness you will be established. You will be far from oppression, for you will not be afraid; and far from terror, for it shall not come near you.
> —Isaiah 54:14 WEB

I boldly declare that I am rooted and established in righteousness. No storm can uproot me, no fear can shake me, and no lie can define me. I stand in divine security because I belong to You. My purpose is preserved in peace, and my destiny is protected from the torment of fear and anxiety.

You have called me into alignment with Your will, and I will not be moved. Every step I take is ordered. Every decision I make is grounded in Your truth. I refuse to be overwhelmed by the pressures of the world, for I am hidden in Your righteousness and shielded by Your grace.

Today, I break agreement with insecurity and confusion. I embrace the peace that surpasses understanding and declare that my atmosphere, my mind, and my future are filled with divine stillness. I walk forward with boldness because You have secured my purpose in righteousness.

In Jesus' name, Amen.

Protection

My Mind is Stayed

> You will keep whoever's mind is steadfast in perfect peace, because he trusts in you.
> —Isaiah 26:3 WEB

I decree that my mind is anchored in You, Lord. I do not entertain the chaos of fear or the distractions of worry. My thoughts are disciplined, fixed, and aligned with Your Word. I dwell in perfect peace because I trust in You completely. You are not just near; You are the Keeper of my soul.

This day will not be hijacked by mental torment or emotional instability. I silence the voice of the accuser and the noise of negativity. I choose to focus on what is lovely, pure, and worthy of praise. Peace is not a fleeting feeling; it is my covenant position.

Surround me, Lord, like walls of fire. Guard my heart and mind from every attack of the enemy. Let Your peace reign over my relationships, my decisions, and my emotions. Because my mind is stayed on You, I walk through this day with calm assurance and divine clarity.

In Jesus' name, Amen.

Provision

Rain of Blessing and Increase

> I will make them and the places around my hill a blessing. I will cause the shower to come down in its season. There will be showers of blessing.
> —Ezekiel 34:26 WEB

I declare that today is drenched in Your goodness. You have opened the heavens over my life, and I am positioned to receive the rain of blessing. Let showers fall on my home, my work, my ministry, and my relationships. I welcome divine increase, for You have called this season one of abundance and refreshing.

No longer will I live in drought, delay, or deficiency. I am surrounded by the dew of favor and the downpour of answered prayers. Even the dry places are springing forth with new life. Every seed I've sown in faith is being watered by Your hand and will produce in due season.

Cause everything connected to me to flourish. Make me a blessing in the lives of others, just as You have blessed me. Let my life be marked by supernatural provision, unexplainable increase, and undeniable favor. Today, I stand under the rain of heaven's abundance.

In Jesus' name, Amen.

POSITION

I Know Your Voice

> My sheep hear my voice, and I know them, and they follow me.
> —John 10:27 WEB

I declare that I belong to the Shepherd, and I know His voice. I will not follow the voice of the stranger, nor will I be misled by the noise of the world. I am attuned to the Spirit of God. As I move through this day, I walk with confidence, clarity, and divine discernment.

You call me by name, and I respond with obedience. I am not wandering aimlessly—I am walking in divine instruction. You lead me beside still waters and into green pastures. You position me where Your purpose unfolds and Your presence abides.

Today, I will hear You in the stillness, in the Word, and even in the interruptions. I refuse confusion, and I embrace divine direction. I am marked by intimacy with You. Because I know Your voice, I will not be deceived, delayed, or distracted. I am exactly where I need to be—following the Shepherd who leads me into destiny.

In Jesus' name, Amen.

DAY 7

PRAISE

MY WORSHIP ASCENDS LIKE INCENSE

> Let my prayer be set before you like incense; the lifting up of my hands like the evening sacrifice.
> —Psalms 141:2 WEB

I declare that my praise rises before You as a holy offering. This morning, I don't come with empty words—I come with a heart that burns with reverence, love, and gratitude. Let my worship ascend like sweet incense, filling the atmosphere with a fragrance that draws Your presence near. I offer not just songs, but my surrendered will, my purified motives, and my yielded spirit.

Lord, as I lift my hands and voice, I silence every complaint, fear, and distraction. You are worthy of uninterrupted devotion. Cleanse my heart so that nothing hinders this sacred exchange. Let my praise pierce through heaviness, disarm the enemy, and draw heaven into this day.

I consecrate this morning with intentional adoration. I create an altar in the midst of my schedule and crown You as Lord over every hour. Let my life become a continual prayer, and my day be saturated in divine communion.

In Jesus' name, Amen.

Purpose

Doors Only You Can Open

> "I know your works (behold, I have set before you an open door, which no one can shut), that you have a little power, and kept my word, and didn't deny my name.
> —Revelation 3:8 WEB

I boldly declare that today I walk through divine doors that no man can shut. You have set before me opportunities that align with heaven's blueprint for my life. I will not fear the unfamiliar nor hesitate at the threshold. You are the Keeper of doors, and I trust You to lead me into places prepared for my influence and impact.

Every closed door was Your protection. Every open door is my invitation to purpose. I reject stagnation, fear, and false limitations. You have unlocked pathways that lead to favor, expansion, and breakthrough. I walk forward with confidence, knowing heaven has gone before me.

Let me recognize the doors You've opened and step through them with bold obedience. I decree that this day is full of strategic movement, supernatural favor, and timely access. My purpose is unfolding with power and precision.

In Jesus' name, Amen.

PROTECTION

STRENGTHENED BY INNER POWER

> For this cause, I bow my knees to the Father of our Lord Jesus Christ, from whom every family in heaven and on earth is named, that he would grant you, according to the riches of his glory, that you may be strengthened with power through his Spirit in the inward man;
> —Ephesians 3:14-16 WEB

I declare that today I am fortified by the strength of Your Spirit in my inner man. I am not weak, I am not wavering—I am rooted in supernatural might that comes from the depths of Your glory. I will not be moved by external pressures, because I am anchored internally by the presence of God within me.

Holy Spirit, infuse every part of my being with power that surpasses human limitation. Let boldness rise where fear once lived. Let stability come where anxiety once reigned. I receive divine strength to overcome adversity, withstand warfare, and stand firm in every assignment.

My inner man is charged with courage, joy, and faith. I am not relying on my flesh—I am drawing from the unlimited reservoir of Your Spirit. I declare I am shielded, sustained, and empowered to fulfill all that this day demands.

In Jesus' name, Amen.

PROVISION

ANOINTED FOR OVERFLOW

> But you have exalted my horn like that of the wild ox. I am anointed with fresh oil.
> —Psalms 92:10 WEB

I decree that today I walk in supernatural strength and overflow. You have anointed me with fresh oil, and that oil marks me for abundance. I will not run dry, I will not strive—I will flow. Your divine empowerment fuels my purpose, and I step into this day with renewed vitality and overflowing grace.

Every assignment I touch is saturated with Your anointing. My capacity is expanding, my energy is replenished, and my hands are empowered to prosper. I break the limitations of lack and declare that I operate under an open heaven. The oil on my life attracts increase, favor, and divine appointments.

I will not be weary or depleted. I carry the fragrance and evidence of Your presence. This day is drenched in breakthrough because I walk in the overflow of what You've poured into me.

In Jesus' name, Amen.

POSITION

I RISE WITH EAGLE VISION

> But those who wait for Yahweh will renew their strength. They will mount up with wings like eagles. They will run, and not be weary. They will walk, and not faint.
> —Isaiah 40:31 WEB

I declare that I mount up today with renewed strength. I rise above distractions, delays, and doubts with the wings of an eagle. I will not be earthbound by circumstances—I am positioned in the spirit to see from a higher realm. This is my day to ascend into clarity, strategy, and supernatural pace.

I shake off weariness and cast off the weights that tried to hold me back. I wait on You, and in the waiting, You renew me. I no longer run aimlessly—I run with purpose. I no longer walk in confusion—I walk in confidence. I soar into divine momentum.

Elevate my mind, Lord. Elevate my vision. Elevate my response. I am not behind—I am right on schedule, moving in sync with heaven's rhythm. This day, I take my rightful position above the storm, where peace and perspective reign.

In Jesus' name, Amen.

DAY 8

PRAISE

THIS DAY IS DIVINE

> This is the day that Yahweh has made. We will rejoice and be glad in it!
> —Psalms 118:24 WEB

I declare that this is the day You have made, and I choose to rejoice in it with all that I am. I step into this day with thanksgiving in my heart and praise on my lips. Regardless of what lies ahead, I begin with a posture of worship. You are the God of my mornings, the Keeper of my moments, and the Author of every unfolding hour.

I praise You because You've already gone before me. This day is not random—it is filled with divine appointments and sacred opportunities. I bless You for the victories embedded in this day, the peace woven through its moments, and the joy that is my inheritance.

As I lift my voice in praise, I silence every spirit of complaint, distraction, and discouragement. Let the sound of my rejoicing break chains and invite Your glory into every space I enter. I exalt You above the pressures and responsibilities of today. You are worthy of all my praise, now and forever.

In Jesus' name, Amen.

Purpose

I Rise Into Greater Light

> But the path of the righteous is like the dawning light, that shines more and more until the perfect day.
> —Proverbs 4:18 WEB

I boldly declare that my path is shining brighter today than ever before. I am not moving in circles or chasing shadows—I am advancing toward divine destiny. You are the Light that guides me, and with every step I take, clarity is increasing, purpose is unfolding, and my vision is expanding.

I refuse to be stuck in past patterns or dimmed by yesterday's failures. I rise in the revelation that I am a vessel of light, called to impact this world with excellence and truth. As I walk forward, I trust that You are illuminating the next step and refining the way I should go.

Today, I step away from every mindset that dims my progress. I embrace wisdom, discernment, and spiritual insight. My path is established by the Lord, and I will not stumble. I shine because You shine through me, and my influence will grow as I remain aligned with You.

In Jesus' name, Amen.

Protection

The Joy of the Lord Shields Me

> Then he said to them, "Go your way. Eat the fat, drink the sweet, and send portions to him for whom nothing is prepared, for today is holy to our Lord. Don't be grieved, for the joy of Yahweh is your strength."
> —Nehemiah 8:10 WEB

I declare today that the joy of the Lord is my strength and stronghold. I do not face this day weary or defenseless, but covered in supernatural joy that lifts, empowers, and protects me. Every arrow of discouragement is deflected by the shield of joy. Every heaviness must bow.

Your joy fuels my courage and becomes a weapon against fear. In moments of challenge, I will not retreat—I will rejoice. I will not be overwhelmed—I will overflow. I decree that nothing can steal my joy because it is rooted in Your unchanging nature.

As I go through this day, I walk with divine resilience. I laugh without fear of the future. I celebrate in the face of opposition. I dwell securely in the joy that strengthens my body, steadies my heart, and surrounds my life with favor. I am guarded by gladness.

In Jesus' name, Amen.

PROVISION

My Year Is Crowned

> You crown the year with your bounty. Your carts overflow with abundance.
> —Psalms 65:11 WEB

I declare that today is marked by divine provision and overflow. You crown this day, this month, and this year with Your goodness. I walk in the abundance of Your favor and the fatness of Your promise. Every place I step is saturated with Your provision and drenched in supernatural grace.

I command the heavens to release every resource assigned to my destiny. My hands are not empty—my storehouses are being filled. I receive provision not just for survival, but for influence, generosity, and legacy. The pathways of my life drip with abundance, and lack has no place in me.

Even in dry places, You cause springs to break forth. Even in barren spaces, You command fruitfulness. I step into today expecting miracles, increase, and divine connections. Your provision is perfect, timely, and tailored to my purpose.

In Jesus' name, Amen.

Position

I Stand in Your Presence

> You will show me the path of life. In your presence is fullness of joy. In your right hand there are pleasures forever more.
> —Psalms 16:11 WEB

I boldly declare that I am positioned in Your presence, and in You, I find fullness of joy and clarity of direction. I do not wander aimlessly; I am anchored in Your divine counsel. At Your right hand, I access pleasures forevermore—peace, purpose, power, and protection.

This day, I will not be moved by distractions or detours. My confidence is in the nearness of my God. You are my portion and my prize, and I rejoice in the security of Your presence. You lead me with wisdom and surround me with songs of deliverance.

I choose to dwell in the place You have set for me. I will not settle for less than Your best or strive for what is not mine. I embrace my appointed position, knowing that where You place me, You also prosper me. Let my steps reflect the certainty that I am right where I belong—in You.

In Jesus' name, Amen.

DAY 9

PRAISE

LET THERE BE LIGHT

> God said, "Let there be light," and there was light.
> —Genesis 1:3 WEB

I declare that this day begins with divine illumination! I speak light into every area of my life, and I command darkness to flee. Just as You spoke in the beginning, Lord, I echo Your voice today—Let there be light over my thoughts, my words, and my path. I praise You as the God who speaks and things change, the God whose voice breaks through chaos and creates order.

This morning, I rise to honor Your creative power at work in me. Your Word is alive and active, and as I praise You, I align myself with Heaven's frequency. Every lie is exposed by truth. Every shadow is broken by the brilliance of Your glory. You are light, and in You, there is no darkness at all.

I praise You for the power to speak life, vision, and clarity into my circumstances. I partner with You to call forth beauty from void places and brilliance from confusion. You are the Light of my life, and by You I see, move, and overcome.

In Jesus' name, Amen.

Purpose

Blessed in My Going

> You shall be blessed when you come in, and you shall be blessed when you go out.
> —Deuteronomy 28:6 WEB

I boldly declare that my coming in and my going out are blessed. Today, I do not move aimlessly, but purposefully under divine covering and with Heaven's backing. Every step I take is pregnant with promise. I am marked for favor, and I walk in alignment with the destiny You've written for me before time began.

Wherever I go today—physically, spiritually, or emotionally—I carry Your presence. Doors open, atmospheres shift, and purpose is revealed because I walk in covenant blessing. I reject aimlessness and confusion, and I embrace intentionality, movement, and divine timing. I will not be delayed, diverted, or denied.

You are the Author of my journey and the Finisher of my faith. I declare that today is not wasted, but ordered. I am anointed for productivity and influence. Even unexpected turns are under Your sovereign control, and all things are working together for my good and Your glory.

In Jesus' name, Amen.

PROTECTION

STRONG, COURAGEOUS, AND COVERED

> Haven't I commanded you? Be strong and courageous. Don't be afraid. Don't be dismayed, for Yahweh your God is with you wherever you go."
> —Joshua 1:9 WEB

I rise today clothed in strength and courage. I am not afraid, I am not dismayed, for You, Lord, are with me wherever I go. Your presence surrounds me like a shield. Your Word is my sword, and Your Spirit goes before me as my defense. I am bold because You have commanded me to be—this is not suggestion, but divine instruction.

I will not shrink back from what lies ahead. I face this day with faith, knowing that giants fall, walls crumble, and enemies scatter in the presence of the Lord. Fear has no hold on me, and discouragement cannot take root. I stand firm and unshaken, because the God of Angel Armies is on my side.

Your covenant of protection covers me—spirit, soul, and body. I declare that I am safe, secured, and strategically placed under the shadow of Your wings. Every plan of the enemy is exposed and canceled. I move forward with peace, power, and bold obedience.

In Jesus' name, Amen.

PROVISION

PLANTED AND PROSPEROUS

> He will be like a tree planted by the streams of water, that produces its fruit in its season, whose leaf also does not wither. Whatever he does shall prosper.
> —Psalms 1:3 WEB

I declare that I am like a tree planted by rivers of living water—steady, nourished, and fruitful in every season. I am not tossed by winds of lack or drought, for my source is not the world but the Lord of all provision. My roots are deep in Your truth, and I will not be moved.

Today, I receive divine provision—spiritually, emotionally, physically, and financially. What I touch prospers because You have blessed the work of my hands. I do not wither in the heat of trials. I flourish because I remain connected to the Source of all increase. I do not strive—I abide.

I declare supernatural favor over my decisions, my resources, and my relationships. Delays break. Lack dissolves. Doors open. I walk in abundance because I am rooted in Your Word and watered by Your Spirit. I bear fruit that lasts, and I will not be barren in any area of life.

In Jesus' name, Amen.

Position

I Am Called by Name

> But now Yahweh who created you, Jacob, and he who formed you, Israel says: "Don't be afraid, for I have redeemed you. I have called you by your name. You are mine.
> —Isaiah 43:1 WEB

I boldly declare that I am not forgotten—I am chosen, redeemed, and named by God. You, Lord, know me intimately, and You have called me Your own. My identity is secure in You, not in titles, opinions, or circumstances. I am positioned by grace, not striving, and my place in Your plan is sealed by love.

I break agreement with rejection, confusion, and insignificance. I rise in the truth that I am fearfully and wonderfully made. My life is not random; it is marked by Your hand and destined for impact. I walk in confidence because I know who I am and whose I am.

I thank You for calling me by name, for knowing my story, and for weaving purpose into every chapter. Today, I step into divine alignment and take my place in Your Kingdom agenda. I will not shrink, settle, or second-guess. I am named, known, and positioned for such a time as this.

In Jesus' name, Amen.

DAY 10

PRAISE

Joy Comes in the Morning

> Sing praise to Yahweh, you saints of his. Give thanks to his holy name. For his anger is but for a moment. His favor is for a lifetime. Weeping may stay for the night, but joy comes in the morning.
> —Psalms 30:4-5 WEB

I boldly declare that this is the day of divine turnaround. Though the night brought weeping, I arise in the power of joy. I shake off heaviness, silence every lie of the enemy, and lift up my voice to magnify the God of restoration. You have turned my mourning into dancing, and I will not hold back my praise.

This morning, I embrace Your mercy that is new and overflowing. I will not carry yesterday's sorrow into today's victory. I rise with a joyful heart, declaring that joy is not only my portion—it is my weapon. Joy opens doors, breaks chains, and releases fresh strength into my spirit.

Because You are faithful, I will rejoice again and again. Let my praise resound louder than my pain, and let my worship drown out every whisper of fear. I prophesy that today is marked by rejoicing, breakthroughs, and laughter. What once caused tears will now give birth to testimony. In Jesus' name, Amen.

PURPOSE

DAILY BREAD, DIVINE ASSIGNMENT

> Give us today our daily bread.
> —Matthew 6:11 WEB

Today, I align myself with heaven's rhythm and declare that divine provision meets divine purpose. I receive my daily bread—not just sustenance for my body, but the exact wisdom, strength, and strategy I need to fulfill what You've assigned me today. I will not live by distraction, but by intention.

Lord, make me sensitive to what matters most. Feed me with Your truth. Nourish me with Your presence. Empower me to walk in today's purpose without anxiety over tomorrow. I declare that each moment is packed with eternal value, and I will walk it out with focus and joy.

I receive provision for my assignment—open doors, divine connections, and timely resources. I will not strive; I will steward. I will not rush; I will rest in Your perfect plan for this day. My life is a vessel of Your will, and my steps are saturated in destiny.

In Jesus' name, Amen.

PROTECTION

VICTORY IS ALREADY MINE

> But thanks be to God, who gives us the victory through our Lord Jesus Christ.
> —1 Corinthians 15:57 WEB

I arise today declaring that I am covered by victory. I do not fight for victory—I fight from it. Because You have already overcome, I stand bold and fearless, knowing that every battle I face today has been settled in the spirit. No force of darkness can overthrow the triumph I walk in.

Every scheme of the enemy is exposed and defeated. I decree that no weapon formed against me shall prosper. I silence fear, I cancel defeat, and I release a shout of victory over my life, my family, and everything connected to me. The blood of Jesus marks me as untouchable.

I take my place as more than a conqueror. I wear the armor of God and move with divine authority. Every fiery dart is extinguished, and every stronghold is shattered. I am protected by the covenant of Christ and preserved for His purpose.

In Jesus' name, Amen.

Provision

Goodness is Chasing Me

> Surely goodness and loving kindness shall follow me all the days of my life, and I will dwell in Yahweh's house forever.
> —Psalms 23:6 WEB

I decree that I live under the relentless pursuit of divine provision. Your goodness and mercy are not behind me—they are overtaking me. I do not have to strive for blessing; blessing is appointed to find me. Lack must flee, and overflow is my portion today.

I awaken to favor, to increase, to supernatural supply. Let every need in my life be met with more than enough. I call forth financial breakthrough, physical strength, emotional peace, and spiritual abundance. I walk with my head held high because I know that heaven has already made provision for this day.

Because You are my Shepherd, I shall not want. You go before me, You follow behind me, and You dwell within me. I declare my home, my hands, and my heart are fertile ground for increase. Today, miracles of provision manifest without delay.

In Jesus' name, Amen.

Position

My Light Breaks Forth

> Then your light will break out as the morning, and your healing will appear quickly; then your righteousness shall go before you; and Yahweh's glory will be your rear guard.
> —Isaiah 58:8 WEB

I rise today in the brilliance of divine positioning. My breakthrough is not coming—it is breaking forth like the dawn. The darkness that tried to linger has been shattered by Your light. I am not stuck, delayed, or forgotten. I am advancing into my ordained place with clarity and power.

Today, I declare that every area of stagnation receives acceleration. My path is illuminated with divine insight. The light of Your favor surrounds me, and the glory of Your presence goes before me. What was hidden is now revealed, and what was blocked is now opened.

I step into my divine assignment with boldness, knowing that I am not behind time—I am right on schedule. My influence expands, my voice is heard, and my purpose is activated. I am positioned in the light of destiny, and nothing can hold me back.

In Jesus' name, Amen.

DAY 11

PRAISE

AWAKEN MY GLORY, LORD

> Wake up, my glory! Wake up, lute and harp! I will wake up the dawn.
> —Psalms 57:8 WEB

I rise this morning with a song in my soul and a shout in my spirit. I declare that my glory awakens to glorify You, O Lord! My heart is stirred to honor You with everything within me. Before the day unfolds, I lift my voice above distractions, fatigue, or delay and set my atmosphere with praise. I will not be silent; I will exalt You with intentional adoration and joyful expectation.

You have given me breath, and with it I command this morning to respond to Your majesty. Let every fiber of my being echo Your greatness. Let my praise break chains, shift atmospheres, and summon angelic help. I decree that my worship is warfare, and the sound of my adoration pierces the heavens and silences every opposing voice.

Father, let my heart remain steadfast and my lips filled with thanksgiving. No matter what awaits me today, I choose to exalt You first. I take authority over this day by lifting up the name above every name. Let my praise provoke miracles, secure favor, and invite divine alignment. In Jesus' name, Amen.

Purpose

Show Me the Way

> Show me your ways, Yahweh. Teach me your paths. Guide me in your truth, and teach me, For you are the God of my salvation, I wait for you all day long.
> —Psalms 25:4-5 WEB

I boldly declare that today I walk with divine guidance and holy instruction. Lord, I surrender every step, plan, and pursuit into Your hands. Teach me Your ways. Lead me into truth and train my heart to follow Your path without hesitation. You are my compass and my counselor, and I will not move without You.

Open my eyes to see what You see. Remove confusion and silence the noise that would cause misdirection. I refuse to lean on my understanding; I wait upon You with trust and expectation. My desire is not just to go forward, but to go forward with clarity, with Your timing, and by Your Spirit.

Where there are crossroads, give me peace. Where there is uncertainty, release fresh revelation. Today I walk in Your will, protected by Your hand and guided by Your wisdom. Let my obedience unlock divine encounters and strategic elevation. I am in sync with heaven, and nothing can hinder the unfolding of Your plan for me.

In Jesus' name, Amen.

Protection

Trained for Victory

> For who is God, except Yahweh? Who is a rock, besides our God, the God who arms me with strength, and makes my way perfect? He makes my feet like deer's feet, and sets me on my high places. He teaches my hands to war, so that my arms bend a bow of bronze.
> —Psalms 18:31-34 WEB

I rise fully armed and fortified in the strength of my God. I declare that I am not a victim—I am a warrior trained by Your hand. You strengthen me for every battle and equip me for every assignment. My feet are steady, my stance is sure, and my hands are ready for war. Today, I move with confidence, knowing You have empowered me for triumph.

No attack will catch me off guard. I am not exposed or unprotected. You surround me like a shield and teach my spirit how to war in the Spirit. I thank You that every fiery dart is extinguished before it reaches me, and every ambush of the enemy is dismantled before it begins. You have taught me how to advance without fear.

Let Your presence go before me and Your angels be stationed around me. I cancel every trap, delay, and demonic agenda assigned to this day. I declare victory in my mind, my body, my home, and every realm of influence You've given me. The enemy will not prevail—I am covered, equipped, and victorious.

In Jesus' name, Amen.

PROVISION

Heaven's Supply Is Mine

> My God will supply every need of yours according to his riches in glory in Christ Jesus.
> —Philippians 4:19 WEB

I decree that lack has no place in my life, for I am connected to the limitless resources of heaven. Father, You are my Source, and everything I need flows from You. I declare this day is saturated with supernatural provision—spiritual, emotional, physical, and financial. You supply according to Your riches, not my limits, and I receive the abundance of Your storehouse.

I break every agreement with scarcity and step boldly into overflow. I will not worry about what I see in the natural, because I trust the economy of the Kingdom. Doors are opening, contracts are releasing, and opportunities are locating me. I am favored, funded, and fulfilled.

I thank You in advance for divine partnerships, creative ideas, and wise stewardship. Bless the work of my hands and breathe on every seed I've sown. Let my life reflect Your generosity and let Your provision establish my testimony. I walk in sufficiency, and I release anxiety—because You have already made a way.

In Jesus' name, Amen.

Position

I Am Made New

> Therefore if anyone is in Christ, he is a new creation. The old things have passed away. Behold, all things have become new.
> —2 Corinthians 5:17 WEB

I boldly declare that I am not who I was. I am a new creation—washed, transformed, and repositioned by grace. I refuse to live from old labels, past mistakes, or former mindsets. Today, I rise in the identity You have given me: redeemed, righteous, and restored. The old has passed away, and I fully embrace the new.

My thoughts are aligned with Your truth, my heart beats with Your rhythm, and my future is filled with Your purpose. I declare that shame no longer has access, and condemnation has lost its grip. I am seated with Christ and empowered to reign in every sphere of influence You've assigned me.

Let this day reflect the reality of my new position. Let heaven's authority govern my speech, my choices, and my relationships. I will not return to what You delivered me from—I move forward, elevated by Your mercy and anchored in Your love. I stand as a witness of Your transforming power.

In Jesus' name, Amen.

DAY 12

Praise

It Is Good to Praise You

A Psalm. A song for the Sabbath day. It is a good thing to give thanks to Yahweh, to sing praises to your name, Most High; to proclaim your loving kindness in the morning, and your faithfulness every night,
—Psalms 92:1-2 WEB

Father, I begin this day doing what is both right and refreshing—giving You praise. As Psalm 92:1–2 declares, "It is good to praise the Lord and make music to Your name, O Most High, proclaiming Your love in the morning and Your faithfulness at night." I align my heart with heaven and lift up thanksgiving before the day unfolds.

It is good to praise You—not just because You deserve it, but because it reminds me of who You are. You've been faithful through the night, and You awaken me with new mercies. I proclaim Your steadfast love before I hear a word from anyone else. I set the tone of this day with worship.

Let praise shape my perspective. Let gratitude silence complaints. Let my morning be marked by music and my night filled with remembrance. I declare: You are good, and it is good to praise You.

This day begins with joy on my lips and glory to Your name.

In Jesus' name, Amen.

PURPOSE

GUIDED BY HIS EYE

> I will instruct you and teach you in the way which you shall go. I will counsel you with my eye on you.
> —Psalms 32:8 WEB

Lord, I thank You for divine direction. As Psalm 32:8 declares, "I will instruct you and teach you in the way you should go; I will counsel you with My loving eye on you." I am not left to wander—I am led by the One who sees it all.

I surrender my decisions into Your hands. Speak to me with clarity, not confusion. Guide me with peace, not pressure. Your counsel is not cold or distant—it flows from love. You see the road ahead, and You know the way through it. I choose not to rush ahead or lag behind. I walk in step with Your guidance.

Today, I follow Your voice over my feelings, and Your wisdom over my wants. My purpose is preserved because You're watching over me.

I am led, loved, and firmly planted in divine purpose.

In Jesus' name, Amen.

PROTECTION

DRESSED FOR VICTORY

> Put on the whole armor of God, that you may be able to stand against the wiles of the devil.
> —Ephesians 6:11 WEB

Mighty God, I put on Your armor this morning. As Ephesians 6:11 commands, "Put on the full armor of God, so that you can take your stand against the devil's schemes." I don't enter this day unaware or unarmed—I am fully covered in Your protection.

I wear truth like a belt. I place righteousness over my heart. I step with readiness to proclaim the Gospel of peace. I carry faith like a shield, and stand in salvation. I take up the sword of the Spirit—Your living Word. No plot of the enemy will catch me off guard. No attack will catch me exposed.

I stand—not in fear, but in faith. Not in weakness, but in the strength of the Lord. I declare that today is a day of victory, not vulnerability.

I am armed, alert, and advancing in divine protection.

In Jesus' name, Amen.

PROVISION

No Good Thing Withheld

> For Yahweh God is a sun and a shield. Yahweh will give grace and glory. He withholds no good thing from those who walk blamelessly.
> —Psalms 84:11 WEB

Faithful Provider, I rest in the beauty of Psalm 84:11: "For the Lord God is a sun and shield; the Lord bestows favor and honor; no good thing does He withhold from those whose walk is blameless." You are both my Source and my covering, and I trust Your heart.

I believe that You do not withhold blessings—I believe You release them in perfect timing. I declare that I walk in favor, clothed in honor, and surrounded by opportunities crafted by Your hand. Every good thing assigned to my life will come forth. I reject envy and embrace contentment, knowing that You will never forget to bless Your own.

Let my steps align with integrity. Let my hands stay open. I walk forward today expecting goodness, because You are the Giver of every good thing.

Nothing lacking. Nothing withheld. Only grace flowing.

In Jesus' name, Amen.

Position

Let My Light Shine

> You are the light of the world. A city located on a hill can't be hidden. Neither do you light a lamp, and put it under a measuring basket, but on a stand; and it shines to all who are in the house. Even so, let your light shine before men; that they may see your good works, and glorify your Father who is in heaven.
> —Matthew 5:14-16 WEB

Lord Jesus, I accept my position and responsibility today. As Matthew 5:14–16 declares, "You are the light of the world… let your light shine before others, that they may see your good deeds and glorify your Father in heaven." I will not hide what You've placed in me.

Let my words bring clarity. Let my actions reflect compassion. Let every room I enter be brighter because I showed up filled with You. I do not shrink back—I shine. I do not boast in my own name—I glorify Yours. I am a city on a hill, not to be hidden but to be used.

Today, use my life to point others toward You. May light silence darkness and love break through coldness.

I shine with heaven's glow—for Your glory alone.

In Jesus' name, Amen.

DAY 13

Praise

I Rise Early to Seek You

> I rise before dawn and cry for help. I put my hope in your words.
> —Psalms 119:147 WEB

Father, before the noise of the day begins, I come to seek You. As Psalm 119:147 declares, "I rise before dawn and cry for help; I have put my hope in Your word." My praise rises before the sun. My heart awakens to worship before the world pulls for my attention.

You are my help, my hope, and my hiding place. I don't wait for crisis to call on You—I come early. I come ready. I come hungry for Your voice and steady in my expectation. Your Word gives me life. Your presence sets my course.

Let my early cry reach Your throne. Let this morning be saturated in Your peace and filled with songs of deliverance. My day is grounded in praise because my trust is anchored in You.

I rise today with worship on my lips and hope in my heart.

In Jesus' name, Amen.

Purpose

This Is the Way, Walk In It

> And when you turn to the right hand, and when you turn to the left, your ears will hear a voice behind you, saying, "This is the way. Walk in it."
> —Isaiah 30:21 WEB

Faithful Shepherd, I thank You for divine direction. As Isaiah 30:21 promises, "Whether you turn to the right or to the left, your ears will hear a voice behind you, saying, 'This is the way; walk in it.'" I will not move in confusion today—I will move by Your voice.

Open my ears to hear clearly. Drown out the noise of doubt, fear, and human opinion. Let every step I take today be in step with Your instruction. Speak to me in moments both quiet and loud—through Your Word, through wisdom, through peace. I declare that I will not walk aimlessly—I walk purposefully.

I don't need all the answers; I just need Your direction. Guide me in clarity and confidence.

Today, I walk in alignment with heaven's voice.

In Jesus' name, Amen.

PROTECTION

MIGHTY THROUGH GOD

> For though we walk in the flesh, we don't wage war according to the flesh; for the weapons of our warfare are not of the flesh, but mighty before God to the throwing down of strongholds,
> —2 Corinthians 10:3-4 WEB

Warrior God, I take my stand today in Your strength. As 2 Corinthians 10:4 declares, "The weapons of our warfare are not carnal but mighty through God to the pulling down of strongholds." I do not fight today in my own power—I fight clothed in Yours.

I speak to every stronghold in my life and declare it must come down—every lie, every fear, every chain of the past. I dismantle them by the truth of Your Word and the authority of the name of Jesus. I don't just defend myself—I take territory.

Let every scheme of the enemy be shattered. Let every high thing that exalts itself against Your knowledge be brought low. I stand guarded and victorious—not in flesh, but in Spirit.

Today, I fight with weapons that win.

In Jesus' name, Amen.

PROVISION

THE WINDOWS OF HEAVEN ARE OPEN

> Bring the whole tithe into the storehouse, that there may be food in my house, and test me now in this," says Yahweh of Armies, "if I will not open you the windows of heaven, and pour you out a blessing, that there will not be room enough for.
> —Malachi 3:10 WEB

Jehovah Jireh, I trust in Your promise today. As Malachi 3:10 says, "Bring the whole tithe into the storehouse… and see if I will not throw open the floodgates of heaven and pour out so much blessing that there will not be room enough to store it." I walk in covenant and expect blessing.

You are not a man that You should lie. What You have spoken, You will perform. I bring to You what is Yours and receive from You what overflows. Let the windows of heaven be opened over my life—over my home, my business, my ministry, my relationships.

Rebuke the devourer. Cancel the curse. Release abundance—not just for me, but through me. I will be a vessel of generosity because You are the God of more than enough.

I live today under an open heaven.

In Jesus' name, Amen.

POSITION

I AM SET APART TO SHINE

> But you are a chosen race, a royal priesthood, a holy nation, a people for God's own possession, that you may proclaim the excellence of him who called you out of darkness into his marvelous light:
> —1 Peter 2:9 WEB

Holy Father, I take hold of who You say I am. As 1 Peter 2:9 declares, "But you are a chosen generation, a royal priesthood, a holy nation, His own special people, that you may declare the praises of Him who called you out of darkness into His marvelous light." I am not ordinary—I am marked by heaven.

You've called me out of darkness, and I will not return to it. I walk in light, speak with boldness, and live with purpose. I am royalty—not by bloodline, but by adoption. I belong to You, and that settles my identity.

Let my life declare Your goodness today. Let my decisions reflect that I'm set apart. I don't strive to fit in—I stand to shine.

I am chosen, royal, and radiant with Your glory.

In Jesus' name, Amen.

DAY 14

PRAISE

I Will Sing of Your Strength

> But I will sing of your strength. Yes, I will sing aloud of your loving kindness in the morning. For you have been my high tower, a refuge in the day of my distress.
> —Psalms 59:16 WEB

Mighty God, I rise this morning with a song in my soul. As Psalm 59:16 declares, "But I will sing of Your strength, in the morning I will sing of Your love; for You are my fortress, my refuge in times of trouble." Before anything unfolds, I declare Your power and rejoice in Your love.

You have been my refuge time and time again. You've shielded me when I was weak and lifted me when I was low. You are my stronghold, my safe place, my hiding place. My morning begins with melody, not murmuring—because You are faithful.

Let my praise fill the atmosphere of my home. Let the song of the Lord silence every shadow. I don't sing because everything is perfect—I sing because You are. Your love is unchanging, and Your strength is unshakable.

This morning, I sing of Your strength and celebrate Your steadfast love.

In Jesus' name, Amen.

PURPOSE

COMMIT AND SUCCEED

> Commit your deeds to Yahweh, and your plans shall succeed.
> —Proverbs 16:3 WEB

Lord, I surrender my plans to You. As Proverbs 16:3 instructs, "Commit to the Lord whatever you do, and He will establish your plans." I release every goal, deadline, and dream into Your hands and ask You to shape it by Your wisdom.

I will not move in pride or self-reliance. I place my desires before You, and I trust that You will align them with Your purpose. Let every decision today flow from dependence on You. Let my work be fruitful because it is founded in surrender.

Even if You change the direction, I will follow. Even if You stretch the timeline, I will trust. I commit it all—my time, my energy, my vision—to You, and I believe You will bring it to completion.

Today, I walk in peace because my plans are in Your hands.

In Jesus' name, Amen.

Protection

Greater Is He Within Me

> You are of God, little children, and have overcome them; because greater is he who is in you than he who is in the world.
>
> —1 John 4:4 WEB

Almighty God, I stand in the truth of 1 John 4:4: "You, dear children, are from God and have overcome them, because the One who is in you is greater than the one who is in the world." I am not intimidated by what's around me—I'm empowered by who is within me.

The greater One lives in me. I will not fear opposition, deception, or spiritual attacks. I overcome because Christ lives in me. Let every lie be silenced. Let every threat fall powerless. Let every force of darkness recognize the authority of Jesus residing in me.

I don't fight alone. I stand in victory before the battle even begins. I declare that the greater power prevails. I am covered, confident, and courageous—not because of my strength, but because of Yours.

Today, I walk fearless—because Greater is He within me.

In Jesus' name, Amen.

PROVISION

THE POWER TO PRODUCE WEALTH

> But you shall remember Yahweh your God, for it is he who gives you power to get wealth; that he may establish his covenant which he swore to your fathers, as it is today.
> —Deuteronomy 8:18 WEB

Father, I acknowledge that everything I have—and all I can achieve—comes from You. As Deuteronomy 8:18 reminds me, "But remember the Lord your God, for it is He who gives you the ability to produce wealth." I do not trust in money—I trust in the One who gives power to create it.

You are the source of every idea, every opportunity, every open door. I thank You for gifting me with creativity, favor, and diligence. Bless the work of my hands today. Breathe on my efforts. Open doors I could never open. Multiply what I steward.

I declare financial wisdom and supernatural strategy. I will not chase riches—I will walk in purpose, and provision will follow. You give the ability, and I honor You with the fruit.

This morning, I walk in covenant prosperity—empowered to produce for Your glory.

In Jesus' name, Amen.

POSITION

I LIVE BY FAITH IN THE SON OF GOD

> I have been crucified with Christ, and it is no longer I that live, but Christ lives in me. That life which I now live in the flesh, I live by faith in the Son of God, who loved me, and gave himself up for me.
> —Galatians 2:20 WEB

Lord Jesus, today I anchor my identity in You. As Galatians 2:20 declares, "I have been crucified with Christ and I no longer live, but Christ lives in me. The life I now live in the body, I live by faith in the Son of God, who loved me and gave Himself for me." My old life is gone—my new life is found in You.

I am not defined by yesterday's mistakes or today's challenges. I am alive with purpose because You live in me. Let my thoughts, choices, and actions reflect the truth that I carry the presence of the Living Christ.

I live by faith—not fear. I move with confidence—not condemnation. I am loved, redeemed, and fully accepted in You. Let the world see Jesus through me today.

This life is Yours. I live it by faith, for Your glory.

In Jesus' name, Amen.

DAY 15

PRAISE

FROM SUNRISE TO SUNSET

> From the rising of the sun to the going down of the same,
> Yahweh's name is to be praised.
> —Psalms 113:3 WEB

Father, I lift Your name high this morning. As Psalm 113:3 declares, "From the rising of the sun to the place where it sets, the name of the Lord is to be praised." From the beginning of this day to its very end, You are worthy of worship.

I don't wait for a good moment to praise You—I declare Your goodness from the moment I rise. You are faithful at dawn and faithful at dusk. I choose to exalt You above every situation and declare that Your name will be honored in my thoughts, my words, and my actions today.

Let praise frame my perspective. Let worship order my steps. Let thanksgiving overflow in every season and every task. From sunrise to sunset, may Your name be lifted up through my life.

This morning, I praise You without delay and without limits.

In Jesus' name, Amen.

Purpose

Establish the Work of My Hands

> Let the favor of the Lord our God be on us; establish the work of our hands for us; yes, establish the work of our hands.
> —Psalms 90:17 WEB

Lord, I invite You into everything I do today. As Psalm 90:17 declares, "May the favor of the Lord our God rest on us; establish the work of our hands for us—yes, establish the work of our hands." I don't want busyness—I want purpose. I ask You to bless what I put my hands to.

Let Your favor rest on every assignment, every meeting, every task, every interaction. I don't strive for success in my own strength; I rely on Your grace to make it fruitful. I surrender both the outcome and the process into Your hands.

Cause my work to endure. Let it reflect Your excellence. Let it be useful, eternal, and full of life. I don't want to simply go through the motions—I want what I do to matter.

Establish the work of my hands today, Lord.

In Jesus' name, Amen.

PROTECTION

MORE THAN A CONQUEROR

> No, in all these things, we are more than conquerors through him who loved us.
> —Romans 8:37 WEB

Mighty God, I rise with confidence in Your power. As Romans 8:37 declares, "No, in all these things we are more than conquerors through Him who loved us." I am not merely surviving—I am overcoming. Because of Jesus, I am victorious before the battle even begins.

No matter what confronts me today, I know the outcome: I win in Christ. I reject the spirit of fear and defeat. I will not shrink back or be overwhelmed. You have already secured the victory, and I walk in it.

Let every obstacle become an opportunity for glory. Let every battle reveal Your strength. I am not fighting for victory—I am fighting from it. Loved by God, covered by grace, and strengthened for every challenge.

Today, I walk as more than a conqueror.

In Jesus' name, Amen.

PROVISION

THE BLESSING THAT ADDS NO SORROW

> Yahweh's blessing brings wealth, and he adds no trouble to it.
> —Proverbs 10:22 WEB

Gracious Father, I receive Your blessing today. As Proverbs 10:22 declares, "The blessing of the Lord brings wealth, without painful toil for it." I trust that You are able to provide in ways that bring peace—not pressure, and joy—not striving.

You are not just my Provider, You are my Peace. I thank You for divine opportunities and increase that are free from anxiety, burnout, or manipulation. I will not chase after what You can freely give. I receive provision with rest, not with fear.

Let today be marked by favor and ease in the assignments You've given me. Let the blessing rest on my work and multiply through my stewardship. I declare supernatural release, grace for growth, and peace in prosperity.

The blessing of the Lord is on my life today—and it brings no sorrow with it.

In Jesus' name, Amen.

POSITION

LED BY THE SPIRIT

> For as many as are led by the Spirit of God, these are children of God.
> —Romans 8:14 WEB

Holy Spirit, I submit myself to Your leading today. As Romans 8:14 says, "For those who are led by the Spirit of God are the children of God." I am not led by emotions, pressure, or opinion—I am led by You.

Let me hear Your voice clearly. Let me sense Your nudge, follow Your whisper, and obey without hesitation. I reject confusion and step into alignment. Because I belong to You, I expect divine guidance and supernatural peace.

Let my choices reflect my sonship. Let my movement be Spirit-directed. I walk confidently, not because I know the way, but because I follow the One who does.

Today, I live as a child of God—led, loved, and filled with Your Spirit.

In Jesus' name, Amen.

DAY 16

PRAISE

A Song in the Night

> Yahweh will command his loving kindness in the daytime.
> In the night his song shall be with me: a prayer to the God of my life.
> —Psalms 42:8 WEB

Faithful God, I praise You for Your nearness both in the light of day and in the stillness of night. As Psalm 42:8 declares, "By day the Lord directs His love, at night His song is with me—a prayer to the God of my life." I thank You that even in the quiet hours, You are singing over me.

Let today begin with the sound of worship and end with the melody of Your presence. I declare that Your steadfast love governs my day, and Your joy carries me through the night. I won't be silenced by sorrow or stress—my praise will rise continually.

You are the God of my life, and I will worship You in every season. Whether I wake with joy or sorrow, I will still declare: You are worthy. Let the music of heaven shape my thoughts and stir my soul.

This morning, I sing to the God who sings over me.

In Jesus' name, Amen.

Purpose

My Future Is in Your Hands

> For I know the thoughts that I think toward you," says Yahweh, "thoughts of peace, and not of evil, to give you hope and a future.
> —Jeremiah 29:11 WEB

Father, I thank You for the clarity and comfort of Your promise in Jeremiah 29:11: "For I know the plans I have for you, declares the Lord—plans to prosper you and not to harm you, plans to give you hope and a future." I trust that my life is not random—it is divinely orchestrated.

You are not guessing about my future. You have plans—good ones. Today, I reject fear of the unknown and step confidently into the path You have laid out. I may not know every detail, but I know You—and that is enough.

Let my decisions today reflect hope, not hesitation. Let my words carry vision, not doubt. I am moving forward not in anxiety, but in assurance.

My future is secure in the One who holds it.

In Jesus' name, Amen.

Protection

Trained for Battle, Covered in Grace

By David. Blessed be Yahweh, my rock, who teaches my hands to war, and my fingers to battle:
—Psalms 144:1 WEB

Lord, I thank You for divine readiness. As Psalm 144:1 declares, "Praise be to the Lord my Rock, who trains my hands for war, my fingers for battle." I don't face this day unprepared—You have equipped me for victory.

Strengthen my spirit and steady my hands. Teach me how to fight the battles of life with wisdom, discernment, and authority. I do not rely on flesh—I rely on faith. I declare that I am spiritually alert and divinely trained to overcome whatever rises against me.

Whether the conflict is internal or external, visible or hidden, I fight from a place of victory in You. Let every assignment of the enemy be dismantled. Let every weapon formed be rendered useless.

I'm trained, I'm armed, and I'm covered.

In Jesus' name, Amen.

Provision

Abounding in Every Good Work

> And God is able to make all grace abound to you, that you, always having all sufficiency in everything, may abound to every good work.
> —2 Corinthians 9:8 WEB

Generous Father, I receive the abundance of Your grace today. As 2 Corinthians 9:8 promises, "And God is able to bless you abundantly, so that in all things, at all times, having all that you need, you will abound in every good work." I lack nothing because You provide everything.

Let every need be met—spiritually, emotionally, physically, and financially. You are not the God of barely enough—You are the God of overflow. I trust You to provide not only for me but through me. Make me a vessel of blessing to others.

Let grace abound. Let wisdom increase. Let generosity flow. I walk in the fullness of Your provision, declaring that I have all I need for every assignment You give me today.

Abundance surrounds me because You are with me.

In Jesus' name, Amen.

POSITION

HE WILL FINISH WHAT HE STARTED

> being confident of this very thing, that he who began a good work in you will complete it until the day of Jesus Christ.
> —Philippians 1:6 WEB

Faithful Lord, I rest in the confidence of Philippians 1:6: "Being confident of this, that He who began a good work in you will carry it on to completion until the day of Christ Jesus." What You start, You finish—and You've started something good in me.

I don't have to strive to complete what You've already begun. I simply need to stay yielded, faithful, and full of trust. I will not fear delay, setbacks, or detours—because You are still working, even when I can't see it.

Let this day be marked by progress, not perfection. Help me trust the process. Remind me that I am a work in progress in the hands of a perfect God.

You will finish what You started in me.

In Jesus' name, Amen.

DAY 17

Praise

Come with Joyful Praise

> Oh come, let's sing to Yahweh. Let's shout aloud to the rock of our salvation! Let's come before his presence with thanksgiving. Let's extol him with songs!
> —Psalms 95:1-2 WEB

O Lord, I come this morning with gladness and gratitude. As Psalm 95:1–2 says, "Come, let us sing for joy to the Lord; let us shout aloud to the Rock of our salvation. Let us come before Him with thanksgiving and extol Him with music and song." I will not be silent today—I will lift my voice with joy.

You are the Rock that doesn't move, the God who always saves. I thank You for every victory behind me and every promise before me. I won't wait for perfect conditions—I choose to praise You now. I shout because You're worthy. I sing because You're good.

Let my praise echo louder than my problems. Let thanksgiving lead my heart before any request. I enter this day singing to the One who holds it all together.

Today begins with joy, music, and the sound of thanksgiving.

In Jesus' name, Amen.

Purpose

Fully Pleasing and Fruitful

> For this cause, we also, since the day we heard this, don't cease praying and making requests for you, that you may be filled with the knowledge of his will in all spiritual wisdom and understanding, that you may walk worthily of the Lord, to please him in all respects, bearing fruit in every good work, and increasing in the knowledge of God;
> —Colossians 1:9-10 WEB

Father, I thank You for the clarity of purpose that comes through Your Spirit. As Colossians 1:9–10 declares, I pray to be "filled with the knowledge of His will through all the wisdom and understanding that the Spirit gives," so I may "live a life worthy of the Lord and please Him in every way."

Fill me with divine wisdom today—not just for big moments, but for every decision. I want to live in a way that honors You, not just in words but in action. Let my life bear fruit—visible, lasting, and rooted in Your will.

Help me walk steadily, purposefully, and joyfully in the lane You've assigned. Let every step be aligned with heaven's intention.

Today, I walk in purpose—full of wisdom and fully pleasing to You.

In Jesus' name, Amen.

PROTECTION

FEAR NOT, FOR I AM WITH YOU

> Don't you be afraid, for I am with you. Don't be dismayed, for I am your God. I will strengthen you. Yes, I will help you. Yes, I will uphold you with the right hand of my righteousness.
> —Isaiah 41:10 WEB

Mighty Defender, I rest in the assurance of Your presence. Isaiah 41:10 declares, "So do not fear, for I am with you; do not be dismayed, for I am your God. I will strengthen you and help you; I will uphold you with My righteous right hand."

I reject the grip of fear today. You are with me—not far off, not indifferent, but near and involved. When I feel weak, You strengthen me. When I feel vulnerable, You lift me up. No threat today is greater than Your presence. No challenge is bigger than Your hand.

Let every fear fall away in light of Your nearness. I declare that I am upheld, secured, and surrounded by the strength of God.

Today, I fear nothing, for You are with me.

In Jesus' name, Amen.

PROVISION

PROSPERITY AND HEALTH FOR THE JOURNEY

> Beloved, I pray that you may prosper in all things and be healthy, even as your soul prospers.
> —3 John 1:2 WEB

Heavenly Father, I receive the truth of 3 John 2 over my life today: "Beloved, I pray that you may prosper in all things and be in health, just as your soul prospers." I thank You that prosperity is not just about things—but about wholeness in spirit, soul, and body.

I declare abundance over my mind, peace in my emotions, strength in my body, and overflow in every area You've assigned me to steward. Let me walk in wellness and productivity. Let me serve others out of the abundance You supply.

Bless my steps, my work, and my relationships. I receive health for the journey and provision for the mission.

Today, I prosper in all things—even as my soul prospers.

In Jesus' name, Amen.

POSITION

SET APART FROM THE START

> "Before I formed you in the womb, I knew you. Before you were born, I sanctified you. I have appointed you a prophet to the nations."
> —Jeremiah 1:5 WEB

Sovereign Lord, I thank You that my identity is not an accident. As Jeremiah 1:5 proclaims, "Before I formed you in the womb I knew you, before you were born I set you apart; I appointed you as a prophet to the nations." I was not an afterthought—I was ordained.

You saw me before anyone else did. You chose me before I could choose You. My calling is not based on qualifications, but on Your eternal decision. I embrace the weight and wonder of being set apart by God.

Let me walk with boldness today, knowing I am appointed. Let me speak with courage, knowing I am sent. I am not random—I am positioned by heaven.

Today, I live as one who was known, chosen, and appointed.

In Jesus' name, Amen.

DAY 18

PRAISE

LET MY WORDS BRING YOU JOY

> Let the words of my mouth and the meditation of my heart be acceptable in your sight, Yahweh, my rock, and my redeemer.
> —Psalms 19:14 WEB

Father, as I rise this morning, I dedicate every word and thought to You. As Psalm 19:14 says, "May the words of my mouth and the meditation of my heart be pleasing in Your sight, Lord, my Rock and my Redeemer." Let my praise not just be in song, but in how I speak and think throughout this day.

Let my heart dwell on what is pure, lovely, and true. Let every sentence I speak reflect honor, truth, and love. Let my thoughts be set on You, and may my words build, not break; bless, not curse.

You are my Rock—unchanging and firm. You are my Redeemer—faithful and close. Let my life be a melody that brings You delight.

Today, may everything within me glorify You.

In Jesus' name, Amen.

PURPOSE

CREATED TO DO GOOD

> For we are his workmanship, created in Christ Jesus for good works, which God prepared before that we would walk in them.
> —Ephesians 2:10 WEB

Heavenly Father, I thank You for the purpose woven into my very being. As Ephesians 2:10 declares, "For we are God's handiwork, created in Christ Jesus to do good works, which God prepared in advance for us to do." I am not aimless—I am intentionally designed by You.

Today, let me walk in the good works You have already laid out for me. Let me not chase opportunity, but step into alignment. Fill me with grace to carry out today's assignment with joy, love, and excellence.

I reject every lie that says I'm not enough or I have nothing to offer. I am Your workmanship. I was made for impact.

This day, I move with purpose and on purpose—because You created me for this.

In Jesus' name, Amen.

PROTECTION

THE LORD IS FAITHFUL TO GUARD ME

> But the Lord is faithful, who will establish you, and guard you from the evil one.
> —2 Thessalonians 3:3 WEB

Faithful God, I rest in the assurance of 2 Thessalonians 3:3: "But the Lord is faithful, and He will strengthen you and protect you from the evil one." I do not face this day alone. You are my strength and shield, and I stand secure in You.

Guard my heart from fear. Guard my mind from deception. Guard my path from danger. I trust not in human strength, but in divine faithfulness. Let no weapon formed against me prosper, and let no scheme of the enemy succeed.

You are faithful in every season. You're not just watching over me—You are actively shielding me.

Today, I walk in confidence, knowing that the Lord protects me.

In Jesus' name, Amen.

PROVISION

BREAD FOR TODAY, HARVEST FOR TOMORROW

> He will give the rain for your seed, with which you will sow the ground; and bread of the increase of the ground will be rich and plentiful. In that day, your livestock will feed in large pastures.
> —Isaiah 30:23 WEB

Provider God, I trust in the promise of Isaiah 30:23: "He will also send you rain for the seed you sow in the ground, and the food that comes from the land will be rich and plentiful." You bless both my sowing and my reaping. You supply seed and provide harvest.

Today, I thank You for the provision already on the way. I sow in faith, with expectancy, knowing that You water what I plant. Let every effort yield increase. Let every act of obedience bear fruit. Provide what I need for this day and pour rain on what I invest for tomorrow.

Let Your blessing rest on the work of my hands and the intentions of my heart.

Today, I walk in the flow of divine provision—fresh rain and abundant harvest.

In Jesus' name, Amen.

Position

Wonderfully Made and Fully Known

> I will give thanks to you, for I am fearfully and wonderfully made. Your works are wonderful. My soul knows that very well.
> —Psalms 139:14 WEB

Creator God, I thank You for the truth of Psalm 139:14: "I praise You because I am fearfully and wonderfully made; Your works are wonderful, I know that full well." I am not flawed in design—I am full of divine purpose.

Let every part of me—body, soul, and spirit—agree with the beauty of Your creation. I am not an accident. I am not overlooked. I am handcrafted by the God of all wisdom. I embrace my worth, not based on appearance or opinion, but on Your Word.

Let me walk in confidence, rooted in my identity in You. Use my uniqueness for Your glory.

Today, I live fully known, fully loved, and wonderfully made.

In Jesus' name, Amen.

DAY 19

PRAISE

I Wait with Worship

> My soul longs for the Lord more than watchmen long for the morning; more than watchmen for the morning.
> —Psalms 130:6 WEB

I rise this morning declaring: My soul waits on the Lord, and my praise rises with the dawn! As Psalm 130:6 says, "My soul waits for the Lord more than watchmen wait for the morning." Lord, I don't just wait passively—I wait with praise. Like the watchman scanning the horizon for first light, my heart leans in with hope, my spirit stretches forward in trust.

Even in silence, You are working. Even in delay, You are faithful. I will not fill my waiting with worry—I will fill it with worship. Let the longing of my soul become a song. Let my trust in You be louder than my timeline. You are worth the wait, and Your timing is always perfect.

Today, I watch with expectation, and I worship with joy.

In Jesus' name, Amen.

Purpose

I Commit and Advance

> Commit your way to Yahweh. Trust also in him, and he will do this:
> —Psalms 37:5 WEB

Today, I declare: My path is not random—my purpose is being fulfilled! Psalm 37:5 says, "Commit your way to the Lord; trust in Him and He will do this." So, Father, I place every plan, every step, every unknown squarely into Your hands. I won't carry the weight of outcomes—I commit the way.

I trust You to establish what You have ordained. Even if I can't see the next step, I know the One who goes before me. Align my desires with Your design. I release control and receive clarity. Today is not just another day—it is a step forward in the purpose You've assigned me.

I commit it. I trust You. And I walk forward with faith.

In Jesus' name, Amen.

Protection

My Refuge Is Near

For the Chief Musician. By the sons of Korah. According to Alamoth. God is our refuge and strength, a very present help in trouble.
—Psalms 46:1 WEB

Lord, I declare boldly: I will not fear, for God is with me! Psalm 46:1 assures me, "God is our refuge and strength, an ever-present help in trouble." You are not distant. You are not delayed. You are here—right here in my moment of need.

When trouble rises, You rise higher. When pressure surrounds me, You surround me with peace. You are my refuge when I'm overwhelmed, my strength when I'm worn, and my help before I even cry out. I choose not to panic—I choose to anchor in Your presence.

I am protected not because of my defenses, but because You defend me. I face this day unafraid.

In Jesus' name, Amen.

PROVISION

DELIGHT AND BE SUPPLIED

> Also delight yourself in Yahweh, and he will give you the desires of your heart.
> —Psalms 37:4 WEB

Today, I speak this truth: When I delight in God, He delights in blessing me. Psalm 37:4 declares, "Take delight in the Lord, and He will give you the desires of your heart." I don't chase things—I chase You, and You fulfill what I truly long for.

You know what I need better than I do. As I center my joy in You, You align my desires with Your will and supply from Your abundance. Let my heart find full satisfaction in Your presence. Let my dreams be shaped by Your goodness.

Provision flows where delight abides. So I choose joy. I choose intimacy. I choose to trust that You know how to bless me better than I know how to ask.

I delight in You—and I trust You to provide.

In Jesus' name, Amen.

POSITION

ALL I DO GLORIFIES YOU

> Whatever you do, in word or in deed, do all in the name of the Lord Jesus, giving thanks to God the Father, through him.
> —Colossians 3:17 WEB

Father, I declare: My life today is not random—it's a reflection of Christ in me. As Colossians 3:17 commands, "And whatever you do, whether in word or deed, do it all in the name of the Lord Jesus..." Every word I speak and every action I take today will point back to You.

I don't just carry Your name—I represent it. Let my tone, my choices, my work, and my interactions reflect heaven's character. I'm not here to impress—I'm here to glorify. Let others see Jesus through my service, my joy, my excellence, and my love.

I am not aimless—I am assigned. I am not forgotten—I am commissioned. Today, I live from a place of identity and authority.

Whatever I do, I do it in Your name.

In Jesus' name, Amen.

DAY 20

PRAISE

BLESS THE LORD, O MY SOUL

By David. Praise Yahweh, my soul! All that is within me, praise his holy name!
—Psalms 103:1 WEB

Today I rise with a command to my soul: Bless the Lord! As Psalm 103:1 declares, "Bless the Lord, O my soul; and all that is within me, bless His holy name." I will not begin this day with complaint or distraction—I will begin with reverence and gratitude.

Every part of me—my thoughts, my emotions, my voice—will join in blessing You. You've been faithful through the night, and You are worthy of praise in the morning. I won't forget Your benefits. I won't overlook Your mercy. I stir my spirit to remember and respond with worship.

Let this day echo with thanksgiving. Let everything within me honor the greatness of who You are.

With all that I am, I bless Your holy name.

In Jesus' name, Amen.

Purpose

Light for My Path

> Your word is a lamp to my feet, and a light for my path.
> —Psalms 119:105 WEB

Father, I declare today: I will not walk in confusion, for Your Word is my guide. As Psalm 119:105 says, "Your word is a lamp to my feet and a light to my path." You do not leave me groping in the dark. You light my way, one step at a time.

Let every decision today be grounded in Your truth. Let the light of Your Word expose every lie, clear every doubt, and direct every move. Whether the path is smooth or steep, I trust that You are leading me.

Even when I don't see the whole picture, I walk forward in confidence because You are lighting my next step.

I follow Your Word—and I find my way.

In Jesus' name, Amen.

Protection

Surrounded by the Lord

> As the mountains surround Jerusalem, so Yahweh surrounds his people from this time forward and forever more.
> —Psalms 125:2 WEB

Almighty God, I stand in the safety of Your presence. As Psalm 125:2 proclaims, "As the mountains surround Jerusalem, so the Lord surrounds His people both now and forevermore." I am not exposed—I am encompassed. You are my shield, my defense, and my stronghold.

I thank You that I am wrapped in Your presence today—going before me, standing behind me, and watching over me. No threat can penetrate Your covering. No danger can outrun Your reach. I am not just protected—I am surrounded.

Let fear fall flat. Let peace rise strong. The presence of the Lord encircles me, and that is my confidence.

Today, I walk secure—because I am surrounded by You.

In Jesus' name, Amen.

PROVISION

GIVING UNLOCKS OVERFLOW

> "Give, and it will be given to you: good measure, pressed down, shaken together, and running over, will be given to you. For with the same measure you measure it will be measured back to you."
> —Luke 6:38 WEB

Gracious Father, I step into the promise of Luke 6:38 today: "Give, and it will be given to you. A good measure, pressed down, shaken together and running over..." I declare that generosity is the gateway to overflow.

I give freely—of time, love, resources, and encouragement—knowing that You are the Giver who always multiplies. Let my giving reflect trust, not fear. Let it release harvest, not just meet need. I will not withhold what You've called me to release. As I give, I open the door to divine return.

Let my hands be open. Let my heart be cheerful. And let the overflow come—not just to me, but through me.

I give—and I walk in abundance.

In Jesus' name, Amen.

Position

Being Transformed in Glory

> But we all, with unveiled face seeing the glory of the Lord as in a mirror, are transformed into the same image from glory to glory, even as from the Lord, the Spirit.
> —2 Corinthians 3:18 WEB

Father, I embrace the journey of transformation. As 2 Corinthians 3:18 declares, "We all… are being transformed into His image with ever-increasing glory, which comes from the Lord, who is the Spirit." I am not who I was yesterday—I am being made more like Christ today.

You are shaping me from the inside out. Let my thoughts reflect Your truth. Let my actions reflect Your nature. Let my attitude reflect Your heart. I refuse to settle—I am growing, shifting, becoming. Your Spirit is at work in me, and I welcome the refining.

Let the glory increase—not for my fame, but for Your reflection. From glory to glory, I am changing.

Today, I live as one transformed.

In Jesus' name, Amen.

DAY 21

PRAISE

I WILL BLESS YOU ALWAYS

> *By David; when he pretended to be insane before Abimelech, who drove him away, and he departed.* I will bless Yahweh at all times. His praise will always be in my mouth.
> —Psalms 34:1 WEB

Lord, I begin this day with a loud and unwavering declaration: I will bless You at all times! No matter what comes my way, my praise will not be silenced. You are worthy in the valley and worthy on the mountain. My heart is fixed on Your faithfulness, and my mouth will reflect the gratitude of my soul.

Let the meditation of my heart and the words of my lips continually lift You high. I choose worship over worry and praise over panic. Even when circumstances shift, You remain constant. I will not allow frustration or fatigue to rob You of the glory You deserve. You have been too good, too present, and too powerful for me to be silent.

Let my praise change the atmosphere around me. Let it rise above complaints and silence every whisper of doubt. Today, I walk with a song and a declaration that You are good and Your mercy endures forever.

In Jesus' name, Amen.

Purpose

You Direct My Steps

> A man's heart plans his course, but Yahweh directs his steps.
> —Proverbs 16:9 WEB

Father, I declare today that my heart belongs to You, and my steps are in Your hands. I make plans, I prepare, I envision—but You are the One who establishes my direction. I surrender the illusion of control and invite Your perfect wisdom to lead me.

Order my day according to heaven's agenda. Block what needs to be blocked, and open what needs to be opened. If You shift the route, I'll follow. If You delay the timing, I'll wait. I trust that Your interruptions are often divine redirections.

Let every decision I make today align with Your will. Let me not only move with intention but with obedience. Even when I don't fully understand, I will walk by faith, knowing that Your hand is guiding me through it all.

In Jesus' name, Amen.

PROTECTION

YOU REACH DOWN AND PRESERVE ME

> Though I walk in the middle of trouble, you will revive me. You will stretch out your hand against the wrath of my enemies. Your right hand will save me.
> —Psalms 138:7 WEB

Mighty Defender, I stand firm today in the confidence that no matter how intense the trouble around me, You are with me in the midst of it. When I walk through dark places, You do not leave me there. When danger draws near, so does Your hand of deliverance.

You stretch out Your arm and preserve my life. You lift me above the attacks of the enemy. Fear has no room where Your presence abides. I declare that no threat, no scheme, no trap will prevail because You are the God who shields me on every side.

Let Your strength arise within me and push back every force that comes to steal, kill, or destroy. I do not just survive—I stand in victory. You are not only protecting me, You are perfecting what concerns me.

In Jesus' name, Amen.

Provision

Overflow in Every Area

> Yahweh will grant you abundant prosperity, in the fruit of your body, in the fruit of your livestock, and in the fruit of your ground, in the land which Yahweh swore to your fathers to give you.
> —Deuteronomy 28:11 WEB

God of abundance, I declare that I walk under open heavens today. You are not a God of lack, but a God who delights in prospering Your children. I thank You for the overflow that touches every area of my life—spiritual, emotional, relational, and material.

Let increase come to every place where I've faithfully sown. Let the fruit of obedience and diligence begin to manifest in fresh supply. I receive Your provision, not just for myself, but so I can bless others and reflect Your generosity in the earth.

Multiply my resources, stretch my capacity, and enlarge my borders. May the richness of Your blessing rest on my home, my work, and every assignment You've entrusted to me.

In Jesus' name, Amen.

POSITION

SEATED WITH CHRIST IN AUTHORITY

> ...and raised us up with him, and made us to sit with him in the heavenly places in Christ Jesus,
> —Ephesians 2:6 WEB

Father, I thank You for elevating me to a new position through Christ. I am not bound to earthly limitations—I am seated with Him in heavenly places. I rise today in the authority and identity that You've given me as a child of the King.

Let me live and move from that seat of victory. I refuse to think like a victim when You've made me victorious. I refuse to fight for acceptance when I already belong. I reject every inferior label and embrace my heavenly identity.

Empower me to speak, serve, and stand with confidence. I am not striving to reach a higher place—I am already seated in it. Let every word I speak and every decision I make reflect where I am positioned in You.

In Jesus' name, Amen.

DAY 22

PRAISE

I Enter with Thanksgiving

> Enter into his gates with thanksgiving, into his courts with praise. Give thanks to him, and bless his name.
> —Psalms 100:4 WEB

Father, I step into this new day with intentional gratitude. I don't wait for everything to be perfect—I enter Your presence right now with thanksgiving in my heart and praise on my lips. I choose to acknowledge Your faithfulness before I ask for anything. You've already done enough for me to praise You forever.

Let my heart remain open in worship. Let my attitude reflect the reverence You deserve. No matter what the world throws at me today, I will not forget who You are and what You've done. I thank You for life, for grace, for peace, and for Your abiding presence.

This morning, I don't just come to get something—I come to give You the honor that is due to Your name. My praise will go before me today, making room for joy, clarity, and victory.

In Jesus' name, Amen.

Purpose

You Lead Me to Profit

> Yahweh, your Redeemer, the Holy One of Israel says: "I am Yahweh your God, who teaches you to profit, who leads you by the way that you should go.
> —Isaiah 48:17 WEB

Lord, I declare today that You are the One who teaches me what is best and leads me in the way I should go. I refuse to walk blindly when You've already promised direction. I tune my ears to Your instruction and align my heart with Your plan. I am not led by pressure—I am led by Your peace.

Guide me in the assignments of this day. Let me not waste time, energy, or opportunity. I surrender every decision into Your hands, knowing You are the God who both instructs and increases. You don't just show me the path—You cause it to prosper.

Open my spirit to learn, adjust, and grow. You are my Teacher, my Trainer, my Compass, and my Provider. I trust that wherever You lead, there will be favor, fruit, and fulfillment.

In Jesus' name, Amen.

Protection

Everlasting Arms Hold Me

> The eternal God is your dwelling place. Underneath are the everlasting arms. He thrust out the enemy from before you, and said, 'Destroy!'
> —Deuteronomy 33:27 WEB

Almighty God, I rest in the strength of Your everlasting arms. You are not just near—You are underneath me, carrying me through every storm and shielding me from every threat. I declare today that I am not vulnerable—I am upheld. You are my refuge, and no enemy can outrun Your reach.

When my own strength falters, You do not. You are my eternal safety net, my shelter in every season. Let fear be far from me today, for I am wrapped in the embrace of the Almighty. Nothing surprises You, nothing is stronger than You, and nothing touches me without passing through Your hand.

Thank You for being the God who never drops me. I walk covered, guarded, and confident—because I am held by You.

In Jesus' name, Amen.

Provision

My Storehouses Overflow

> Honor Yahweh with your substance, with the first fruits of all your increase: so your barns will be filled with plenty, and your vats will overflow with new wine.
> —Proverbs 3:9-10 WEB

Gracious Father, I stand in full expectation of divine supply. You have promised that as I honor You, my barns will be filled to overflowing and my vats will brim with new wine. So today, I bring my first and best before You—not just my resources, but my heart, my time, and my obedience.

You are not a God of lack, but of more than enough. I declare that everything I touch today will be saturated in increase—because I move in covenant with the Giver. Let every area where I've sown in faith be met with harvest. Let generosity flow through me, and let favor follow me.

I do not toil for survival—I steward abundance. Thank You for provision with peace and blessing without sorrow.

In Jesus' name, Amen.

POSITION

CHRIST IN ME, MY HOPE

> ...to whom God was pleased to make known what are the riches of the glory of this mystery among the Gentiles, which is Christ in you, the hope of glory;
> —Colossians 1:27 WEB

Jesus, I thank You that You don't just walk beside me—You live within me. This morning, I remember that the mystery and glory of the gospel is Christ in me, the hope of glory. I am not powerless. I am not alone. The very presence of the Living God dwells in me by Your Spirit.

Let that reality shape how I speak, move, and see myself today. I am not trying to become something—I already carry Your presence. Let my life manifest the hope, power, and beauty of the One who lives within. I will not diminish what You've placed inside of me.

I walk in dignity, in confidence, and in holiness—not in my own strength, but because You are within. Let the world see Your glory rising through me today.

In Jesus' name, Amen.

DAY 23

PRAISE

LIGHT HAS COME FOR ME

> ...because of the tender mercy of our God, whereby the dawn from on high will visit us, to shine on those who sit in darkness and the shadow of death; to guide our feet into the way of peace."
> —Luke 1:78-79 WEB

I rise this morning with a shout of praise, for Your tender mercy has visited me like the rising sun breaking through the darkness. You have brought light to every shadowy place in my life, and today I declare that no corner of my heart will remain dim or hidden. I welcome the warmth of Your presence and the clarity of Your guidance as I walk into the light of a new day.

You have not forgotten me, Lord. When I felt lost or unseen, You came with compassion, lighting my path and giving hope to my soul. Your light is not just for direction but for transformation. This morning, I yield to its power to restore, awaken, and elevate every part of me.

Let Your light shine through me as a witness to others still walking in the dark. Make my life a beacon of Your love, drawing the hurting, the weary, and the lost toward You. I will not be silent—I will glorify You for the light that has dawned in my spirit and the peace that now governs my steps. In Jesus' name, Amen.

Purpose

I Ask and Receive Wisdom

> But if any of you lacks wisdom, let him ask of God, who gives to all liberally and without reproach; and it will be given to him.
> —James 1:5 WEB

I declare that I am a seeker of divine wisdom, and today I ask boldly for the insight I need. I will not move through this day in confusion or double-mindedness. You are the God who gives wisdom generously and without reproach. So I open my heart to receive it—clear, unshakable, and tailored for every decision I face.

I silence the noise of human logic and fleeting opinions and tune in to the sound of Your voice. You speak with clarity, and Your counsel never leads astray. Thank You for the wisdom to navigate relationships, assignments, and the hidden details of my day. I refuse to lean on my own understanding; instead, I lean into the limitless mind of Christ within me.

With this wisdom, I move forward in confidence and precision. I will not waste time, energy, or opportunity. I am strategically placed, purposefully equipped, and divinely instructed. I walk into divine appointments and make decisions that align with heaven's plan for me.

In Jesus' name, Amen.

PROTECTION

SURROUNDED BY ANGELIC DEFENSE

Yahweh's angel encamps around those who fear him, and delivers them.
—Psalms 34:7 WEB

I boldly declare that I am divinely protected. Today, I dwell in the safety of Your presence, and I am surrounded by angelic forces assigned to guard, shield, and war on my behalf. I do not walk alone—Your messengers are encamped around me, creating an invisible fortress that no enemy can penetrate.

I refuse to live in fear or anxiety. I will not anticipate danger, disaster, or defeat. My confidence is in You, the God who sees, who knows, and who secures every step I take. You have dispatched heaven's army to protect not only my body but my peace, my purpose, and my promise.

Let every trap set against me be exposed and overturned. Let every fiery dart be extinguished before it reaches its target. I decree divine immunity over my family, my home, my travels, and everything under my care. No harm shall overtake me, because I am covered under the shadow of the Almighty.

In Jesus' name, Amen.

Provision

I Shall Not Lack

> The young lions do lack, and suffer hunger, but those who seek Yahweh shall not lack any good thing.
> —Psalms 34:10 WEB

I rise with the bold assurance that I lack nothing. I am not abandoned, overlooked, or forgotten. You are my Shepherd, my Source, and my Sustainer. Today, I reject the lie of insufficiency and embrace the truth that I will experience divine provision in every area of my life.

Because I seek You first, You cause every good thing to pursue me. I call forth provision—spiritual, emotional, financial, and relational. Doors are opening, answers are coming, resources are being released. Even in lean places, I will be fed. Even in wilderness seasons, You make rivers flow.

I will not be intimidated by rising costs, closed doors, or unmet expectations. I stand on the covenant of Your goodness, knowing that the young may grow hungry, but I will testify of Your faithfulness. I declare that my table is set, my cup is full, and my heart overflows with thanksgiving.

In Jesus' name, Amen.

POSITION

I Am Transformed and Aligned

> Don't be conformed to this world, but be transformed by the renewing of your mind, so that you may prove what is the good, well-pleasing, and perfect will of God.
> —Romans 12:2 WEB

I boldly declare that I will not be conformed to this world's patterns, pressures, or distractions. I am being transformed by the renewing of my mind. Today, I position myself in alignment with the mind of Christ. I cast down every thought that contradicts Your truth and submit fully to the wisdom of heaven.

I choose clarity over confusion, discernment over deception, and purpose over popularity. Let my mindset reflect the Kingdom—bold, obedient, and anchored in righteousness. I refuse to let culture define me; I am shaped by Your Word and positioned for divine impact.

As I renew my mind, I gain access to what is good, acceptable, and perfect in Your will. I walk confidently into every assignment You have prepared. I declare that I am not stuck in cycles or hindered by old patterns. I have the mind of Christ, and with it, I walk in supernatural understanding.

In Jesus' name, Amen.

DAY 24

PRAISE

MY SONG IS MY WEAPON

> Praise Yahweh! Sing to Yahweh a new song, his praise in the assembly of the saints. May the high praises of God be in their mouths, and a two-edged sword in their hand;
> —Psalms 149:1, 6 WEB

I rise today with a new song in my mouth and praise in my heart! I boldly declare that I will not be silent. I will lift up the sound of victory and worship the One who reigns forever. My praise is not optional—it is essential. It aligns me with heaven and confounds the plans of the enemy. I rejoice in You, Lord, not just in private, but in the presence of the faithful, in unity with the redeemed.

My song is my testimony, and my worship is my warfare. I exalt You not based on how I feel, but because You are worthy. Even in trials, I choose to lift my voice. Even in uncertainty, I offer thanksgiving. My praise shifts atmospheres, breaks chains, and releases divine strategies for this day. I will not let my circumstances mute my melody.

You inhabit my praise, and where You dwell, nothing unclean can remain. I welcome Your glory into my morning. I awaken the dawn with my worship, and I crown this day with the sound of triumph. Let every moment be filled with joyful reverence, for You are the King who deserves my continual praise.

In Jesus' name, Amen.

Purpose

Fruitful Because I'm Connected

> I am the vine. You are the branches. He who remains in me, and I in him, the same bears much fruit, for apart from me you can do nothing.
> —John 15:5 WEB

Today I declare that I am fully connected to the true Vine—Jesus Christ, my Source, my Strength, and my Sustainer. I do not operate in my own wisdom, ability, or ambition. Everything I am and everything I do flows from abiding in You. Apart from You, I can do nothing, but in You, I bear much fruit—lasting, eternal, and impactful.

I surrender every branch of my life to Your pruning, knowing that Your refining leads to greater productivity. I cast off dead works and fruitless striving. I yield my gifts, my time, and my thoughts to divine purpose. As I abide in You, clarity comes. Discernment increases. Supernatural alignment takes place. My life becomes a testimony of what happens when heaven partners with humanity.

Let everything I touch today reflect Your presence in me. I speak life into assignments, creativity into tasks, and excellence into responsibilities. I refuse to be barren or busy with no results. Instead, I live from overflow, rooted in grace and grounded in truth.

In Jesus' name, Amen.

Protection

Preserved from Every Evil

> Yahweh will keep you from all evil. He will keep your soul.
> —Psalms 121:7 WEB

I declare today that I am divinely protected. The Lord is my keeper, and no harm shall overtake me. I rest in the assurance that You guard my soul, my going out, and my coming in. There is no moment today when I am uncovered or exposed. You are my shield, my hiding place, and my strong tower.

I renounce every assignment of the enemy, every plan of destruction, every trap of fear. No evil shall approach me, no plague shall touch my dwelling. I plead the blood of Jesus over my body, my family, my finances, and my future. Every arrow sent against me is returned to sender. I stand under the canopy of heaven's defense.

I walk confidently, knowing I am surrounded by angelic assistance and divine surveillance. Nothing can access me without passing through You first. I declare that my mind is guarded, my heart is at peace, and my atmosphere is secured. Today, I walk in divine immunity, protected from all evil, seen and unseen.

In Jesus' name, Amen.

Provision

Beauty for My Ashes

> To appoint unto them that mourn in Zion, to give unto them beauty for ashes, the oil of joy for mourning, the garment of praise for the spirit of heaviness; that they might be called trees of righteousness, the planting of the LORD, that he might be glorified.
> —Isaiah 61:3 KJV

I decree that today is a day of divine exchange. I give You my heaviness, and You clothe me with joy. I release every burden, and You crown me with beauty. I will not live in lack, sorrow, or mourning, because You have declared abundance and restoration over me. You are the God who turns my ashes into something glorious.

Every area of loss is now a place of gain. You anoint me with the oil of gladness, and my dry places begin to flourish. I step into the fullness of provision—not just material, but emotional, spiritual, and relational. You are rebuilding my ruins, refreshing my soul, and reigniting my hope. Where despair tried to root itself, You have planted purpose and praise.

Let my life reflect the richness of Your grace. Let my words be filled with gratitude. I refuse to live as one defeated or depleted. I rise today in the strength of Your abundance, wearing the garments of joy and walking boldly in the fullness of Your promises.

In Jesus' name, Amen.

Position

I Will See God's Goodness

> I am still confident of this: I will see the goodness of Yahweh in the land of the living.
> —Psalms 27:13 WEB

I stand in faith today, declaring that I will see the goodness of the Lord in the land of the living. I am not forsaken, I am not forgotten—I am firmly positioned in the waiting with confident expectation. No matter what surrounds me, I anchor myself in hope. You are good, and Your goodness is chasing me down.

Even when I can't see the outcome, I trust the process. I will not faint. I will not fear. I will not give up. I fix my eyes not on what is seen, but on what You've promised. You are aligning everything for my favor, orchestrating divine moments, and positioning me for breakthroughs I can't yet imagine.

This is not a season of delay, but of preparation. You are strengthening me in the waiting, building my endurance, and sharpening my vision. I will stand still and see the salvation of the Lord. My feet are planted on Your faithfulness, and I will not be moved.

In Jesus' name, Amen.

DAY 25

PRAISE

I Will Bless You Daily

> *A praise psalm by David.* I will exalt you, my God, the King. I will praise your name forever and ever. Every day I will praise you. I will extol your name forever and ever. Great is Yahweh, and greatly to be praised! His greatness is unsearchable.
> —Psalms 145:1-3 WEB

I declare that praise is my daily assignment and my eternal delight. From the rising of the sun to its setting, my mouth will bless You, Lord. I refuse to allow the noise of life to drown out the song of gratitude in my soul. Each day You give me breath is another chance to exalt Your holy name. You are great, and Your greatness is unsearchable.

Today, I choose to magnify You above every situation. I silence the voice of worry and lift up the sound of worship. You are faithful in all Your ways and near to all who call on You in truth. No matter what I face, I will praise You, because You are worthy and You never fail.

Let my praise shift the atmosphere around me and open the heavens over me. Let it create divine alignment and release supernatural favor. As I bless You with my lips, bless me with Your presence, and let Your joy strengthen me throughout this day.

In Jesus' name, Amen.

Purpose

It's All Working for Good

> We know that all things work together for good for those who love God, to those who are called according to his purpose.
> —Romans 8:28 WEB

I declare with confidence that all things are working together for my good, because I love You and am called according to Your purpose. Nothing in my life is wasted—not the pain, the delay, the disappointment, or the detour. You are the Master Weaver, and You are threading every experience into the tapestry of my destiny.

Today, I align my heart with Heaven's perspective. I reject fear and embrace faith. Even when I cannot see the full picture, I trust Your divine strategy. You are the God who redeems moments and multiplies meaning. I will not question what You allow—I will walk in peace, knowing it is preparing me for glory.

Cause every decision I make today to reflect Your wisdom and design. Let every step move me closer to my kingdom assignment. I believe You are causing all things—good, bad, and unexpected—to serve Your purpose in my life.

In Jesus' name, Amen.

Protection

The Lord Is My Safe Place

> Yahweh is good, a stronghold in the day of trouble; and he
> knows those who take refuge in him.
> —Nahum 1:7 WEB

I boldly declare that I am covered by the goodness of God. You, Lord, are my refuge in the day of trouble. When chaos surrounds me, I hide in the cleft of Your presence. You know those who trust in You, and I am counted among them. No danger, disaster, or demonic scheme can penetrate the shield of Your protection.

I cast down fear and anxiety. I dwell under the shadow of the Almighty, and I will not be shaken. You have assigned angels to encamp around me, and Your presence is my stronghold. I am divinely hidden from every trap and attack of the enemy.

Cover my household, my mind, my journey, and my destiny. Let no evil befall me, and no harm come near. I declare divine safety over every area of my life today. I walk boldly and confidently, shielded by the Lord of Hosts.

In Jesus' name, Amen.

PROVISION

Reward Is Coming to Me

> May Yahweh repay your work, and a full reward be given to you from Yahweh, the God of Israel, under whose wings you have come to take refuge."
> —Ruth 2:12 WEB

I declare today that I am under divine reward and recompense. You, O Lord, are the God who sees my faithfulness, and You will not forget my labor of love. I take refuge in You, and You are releasing blessings into my hands. I trust You to honor what I've sown in tears and to multiply what I've given in faith.

You are positioning me for supernatural provision. Just as You orchestrated favor for Ruth, I decree divine appointments and unexpected kindness are meeting me today. My steps are ordered into the right field, at the right time, with the right people. I lack nothing because You are my source.

Let every seed I've planted—through prayer, obedience, or sacrifice—break open with harvest. I call forth the abundance of Heaven to locate me now. Reward is not just coming; it is here. I live under the open hand of a generous God.

In Jesus' name, Amen.

Position

I Walk in the Light

> Again, therefore, Jesus spoke to them, saying, "I am the light of the world. He who follows me will not walk in the darkness, but will have the light of life."
> —John 8:12 WEB

I declare that I no longer walk in darkness or confusion. I follow You, Lord Jesus, and I walk in the light of life. Every shadow of uncertainty is dispelled by Your presence. The path before me is illuminated by truth, and I will not stumble. You are the Light of the world, and I choose to follow You closely today.

I reject every lie that says I am lost or forgotten. I am aligned with divine timing and divine direction. Your light exposes what is hidden, reveals what is real, and guides me into destiny. Today, I will not second-guess myself—I am positioned in clarity and guided by wisdom from above.

Shine through every area of my life. Illuminate my decisions, my relationships, and my opportunities. Let others see Your glory through me as I walk boldly in the identity and authority You've given me. I am a child of the light, and I will never return to darkness.

In Jesus' name, Amen.

DAY 26

PRAISE

I Will Not Be Moved

> I have set Yahweh always before me. Because he is at my right hand, I shall not be moved.
> —Psalms 16:8 WEB

I declare this morning that my eyes are fixed on You, Lord. You are always before me—constant, near, and unshakable. I praise You because You are my anchor in the storm and my joy in the stillness. I will not be moved, because You uphold me with Your righteous hand and steady my soul in every season.

As I lift my voice in worship, my heart aligns with heaven's rhythm. Fear has no place here. Doubt flees as Your presence surrounds me. You are my everlasting peace, and I magnify Your holy name. I praise You not just for what You do, but for who You are—my keeper, my refuge, my source of stability.

Today, my praise becomes my posture. I rejoice with confidence, knowing that You are with me and within me. I stand in victory, because You go before me and remain at my right hand. Let my worship build a dwelling place for You all day long.

In Jesus' name, Amen.

Purpose

He Leads Me Forward

> He restores my soul. He guides me in the paths of righteousness for his name's sake.
> —Psalms 23:3 WEB

This morning, I declare that I am not lost—I am led. You, O Lord, are the Shepherd of my soul, and You guide me with clarity and care. I trust Your direction over my assumptions, Your timing over my urgency, and Your path over my preference. You restore my soul and lead me into righteousness for Your glory.

Even when the way is unfamiliar, I choose to follow. I release control, striving, and confusion, because Your leadership is perfect. I am not wandering—I am walking in divine alignment with Heaven's blueprint for my life. Every step is ordered, and every pause is purposeful.

Let this day unfold with intentional movement and Spirit-led decisions. May Your name be glorified in every action I take. Use me as a vessel of purpose, and let my life bear fruit that honors You.

In Jesus' name, Amen.

Protection

You Are My Saving Strength

> Yahweh, the Lord, the strength of my salvation, you have covered my head in the day of battle.
> —Psalms 140:7 WEB

I rise this morning declaring that You are my deliverer and my saving strength. You cover my head in battle and shield my heart from fear. You are the One who protects me from hidden traps and seen enemies. I do not enter this day unarmed—Your presence is my defense and Your Word my weapon.

I refuse to be intimidated by the threats of the enemy. You have already declared victory over every scheme set against me. I put on the whole armor of God and stand secure in the knowledge that I am covered by divine protection. The fiery darts of the wicked cannot touch me, because You are my shield.

Guard my thoughts, my conversations, and every place my feet will tread today. Assign angels to encamp around me and my household. Let no harm befall me, and let every weapon formed against me be rendered powerless.

In Jesus' name, Amen.

Provision

I Am Blessed to Bless

> I will make of you a great nation. I will bless you and make your name great. You will be a blessing.
> —Genesis 12:2 WEB

I declare today that I walk under an open heaven. You have made me into a vessel of blessing, and Your favor surrounds me like a shield. I am not just receiving—I am releasing. You have chosen to bless me so I may bless others, to increase me so I may be generous, and to elevate me so I may glorify You.

This morning, I align with the covenant of increase. I thank You for divine connections, creative ideas, and supernatural supply. I am not bound by lack or limited by what I see. You are my Source, and from Your hand flows everything I need—resources, relationships, and opportunities.

Let every gift You've placed in me be fruitful today. I decree that my life multiplies, overflows, and pours into others. Make me a distribution center of Your goodness and glory.

In Jesus' name, Amen.

Position

Filled With Hope and Power

> Now may the God of hope fill you with all joy and peace in believing, that you may abound in hope, in the power of the Holy Spirit.
> —Romans 15:13 WEB

I declare this morning that I am filled with fresh hope, supernatural joy, and divine power. My position is not defined by circumstances but by the God of hope who fills me with overflowing confidence. I am not depleted—I am strengthened. I do not waver—I abound in hope by the power of the Holy Spirit.

Today, I step forward rooted in who I am in Christ. I cast off the weight of disappointment and clothe myself in expectation. You are the lifter of my head, the sustainer of my heart, and the One who positions me for impact and influence.

Let my life radiate the evidence of Your power. I will not shrink back. I rise in faith, joy, and the bold assurance that what lies ahead is greater than what's behind me. I take my seat in heavenly places and walk in the authority You've given me.

In Jesus' name, Amen.

DAY 27

PRAISE

A NEW SONG ARISES

> Sing to him a new song. Play skillfully with a shout of joy!
> —Psalms 33:3 WEB

I rise today with a heart bursting with praise! I will not offer You stale worship or recycled words—I bring You a new song, fresh from my spirit, born from the revelation of Your faithfulness. You are worthy of my most excellent praise. My voice, my rhythm, my melody are instruments of glory. I sing with passion, not performance, because You deserve my best offering.

I worship not for what I can get, but because of who You are—holy, majestic, and magnificent beyond comprehension. As I lift this new song, may the atmosphere around me shift. Let heaven respond and earth align with the sound of true worship. My praise tears down strongholds, breaks barriers, and summons the presence of God.

This morning, I don't just sing—I prophesy with melody, I declare with rhythm, and I exalt with excellence. Let my praise be heard in heaven and felt in the earth. I declare this day is anointed because I have chosen to begin it with worship.

In Jesus' name, Amen.

Purpose

Fully Equipped for Every Assignment

> Now may the God of peace, who brought again from the dead the great shepherd of the sheep with the blood of an eternal covenant, our Lord Jesus, make you complete in every good work to do his will, working in you that which is well pleasing in his sight, through Jesus Christ, to whom be the glory forever and ever. Amen.
> —Hebrews 13:20-21 WEB

I boldly declare that I am fully equipped for every good work You've ordained for me today. Your hand has shaped me, Your Spirit empowers me, and Your Word directs me. I will not step into this day unprepared or unsure. You have made me complete in every way necessary to carry out Your will with confidence and precision.

Every tool I need, every door I require, every resource I lack—You are supplying it even now. I refuse to walk in fear or hesitation. I embrace divine assignments with joy, knowing You work in me both to will and to do for Your good pleasure. My life is an expression of Your grace and excellence.

Order my moments, align my relationships, and sharpen my discernment. Let divine timing, divine wisdom, and divine favor follow me. I surrender my will so Your purpose can prevail. I am not just moving—I am being moved by You.

In Jesus' name, Amen.

PROTECTION

SAFE IN YOUR STRONG TOWER

> Yahweh's name is a strong tower: the righteous run to him, and are safe.
> —Proverbs 18:10 WEB

I declare that I am hidden in You, the name above every name. I run to You today, my strong tower and unshakable fortress. Though chaos may surround me and threats may rise, I remain unmoved. Your name is my covering, and Your presence is my shield. I do not fear the unknown, for I am wrapped in the known security of who You are.

Every arrow aimed at me is intercepted. Every plan of the enemy is dismantled. I dwell under divine protection—not because I deserve it, but because I am in covenant with a faithful God. I silence every voice of fear and stand on the truth that I am guarded by heaven's armies.

Today, I walk with confidence. No accident, scheme, or ambush will touch me or my household. I activate angelic assistance and divine defense. My steps are ordered, my path is secure, and my soul is at peace.

In Jesus' name, Amen.

PROVISION

FAVOR FOLLOWS ME EVERYWHERE

> But Yahweh was with Joseph, and showed kindness to him, and gave him favor in the sight of the keeper of the prison.
> —Genesis 39:21 WEB

I boldly declare that favor follows me today—relentlessly, abundantly, and without fail. Just as You were with Joseph in every season, You are with me now. In the midst of lack, I experience overflow. In unfamiliar places, I walk in undeniable grace. Your presence opens doors no man can shut and causes me to prosper where others perish.

I thank You for the evidence of Your mercy. Even when circumstances seem unfavorable, Your hand rests upon me. Let divine influence go before me in meetings, decisions, and negotiations. Cause those in authority to show me kindness beyond understanding, not because of who I am, but because of who You are within me.

Provision is not my pursuit—Your presence is. And wherever You are, abundance dwells. I will not strive, fear, or beg. I walk in peace, knowing You are the God who supplies all my needs according to Your riches in glory.

In Jesus' name, Amen.

POSITION

WALKING FULLY IN THE LIGHT

> But if we walk in the light, as he is in the light, we have fellowship with one another, and the blood of Jesus Christ, his Son, cleanses us from all sin.
> —1 John 1:7 WEB

I rise this morning with clarity and confidence, knowing I am positioned in the light of Your truth. No shadow of shame or cloud of confusion can follow me. I walk in fellowship with You, Lord, and that fellowship illuminates my identity, my direction, and my destiny. I refuse to hide or diminish my light. I step into today fully exposed to Your righteousness and fully covered by Your grace.

Every lie that once held me captive is broken by the power of the light I now live in. I am not chasing purpose—I am aligned with it. Your truth sets my internal compass and keeps me from drifting. I do not stumble, for Your light reveals what's ahead and guards what's behind.

Let my presence today be a reflection of Your brilliance. Let my words carry light, my decisions be guided by light, and my relationships be nurtured in light. I am not lost, hidden, or forgotten. I am seen, known, and strategically placed in this moment for Your glory.

In Jesus' name, Amen.

DAY 28

PRAISE

MY STRENGTH AND MY SONG

> Yah is my strength and song. He has become my salvation. This is my God, and I will praise him; my father's God, and I will exalt him.
> —Exodus 15:2 WEB

I declare with boldness this morning that You, O Lord, are my strength and my song. You have become my salvation, and I lift my voice to exalt You. You are the One who lifts me when I'm weary, who steadies me when I stumble, and who surrounds me with songs of deliverance. I praise You not from routine but from deep gratitude—because You have done mighty things for me.

You are the God who parts the waters and brings me through every trial with victory. I will not be silent, for You deserve the highest praise. You are my refuge in battle, my melody in the midnight hour, and the One who has turned my mourning into dancing. My worship rises like incense and shifts the atmosphere around me.

I sing not only because of what You've done, but because of who You are—mighty, faithful, and ever-present. Let my life today become a living praise, a walking testimony of Your power and goodness. You are worthy, and I glorify Your name with every breath. In Jesus' name, Amen.

Purpose

Guided by the Lord Continually

> and Yahweh will guide you continually, and satisfy your soul in dry places, and make your bones strong; and you shall be like a watered garden, and like a spring of water, whose waters don't fail.
> —Isaiah 58:11 WEB

This day, I declare that my life is not aimless—I am led by the Lord continually. You are the One who satisfies my soul in dry places and strengthens me when I feel depleted. You make me like a well-watered garden, flourishing even when others wither. My purpose is not limited by my surroundings; it is sustained by Your Spirit.

Lead me in every decision, Lord. Whisper Your wisdom into my spirit. Cause divine connections to locate me and divine strategy to fill my mind. I will not lean on my own understanding, for You are the One who establishes my steps. I will fulfill the assignment written in Your book for me today.

Even when the way seems unclear, I trust Your hand to guide me. I am aligned with heaven's agenda and filled with purpose-driven passion. Use me today to bring life, healing, and light to others. I move forward knowing that You are with me and that my destiny is unfolding by design.

In Jesus' name, Amen.

Protection

Fearless in the Light

By David. Yahweh is my light and my salvation. Whom shall I fear? Yahweh is the strength of my life. Of whom shall I be afraid?
—Psalms 27:1 WEB

I rise today with fearless confidence, for You are my light and my salvation. No darkness can overpower me, no enemy can intimidate me, because I am hidden in the shelter of the Most High. You are the strength of my life, and I will not be shaken.

Though challenges may arise, I will not cower in fear. You are the One who defends, delivers, and shields me. Your light surrounds my path, and Your presence is my hiding place. I decree that no weapon formed against me shall prosper and no plan of the enemy will succeed. I am covered—body, soul, and spirit.

Today, I walk in peace and holy boldness. I step into my assignments knowing that I am divinely guarded. Every arrow sent against me returns to its sender. Every snare set before me is exposed and dismantled. I will not be afraid of sudden terror, for the Lord is my covering.

In Jesus' name, Amen.

PROVISION

LIFTED AND SUPPLIED BY GOD

> Kings shall be your foster fathers, and their queens your nursing mothers. They will bow down to you with their faces to the earth, and lick the dust of your feet; Then you will know that I am Yahweh; and those who wait for me shall not be disappointed."
> —Isaiah 49:23 WEB

Today, I declare that I look not to man, but to You, my Source and Sustainer. You are the God who lifts me, who provides for me, and who causes kings and nations to serve Your purpose in my life. I receive divine supply for every need—spiritually, emotionally, financially, and physically.

You have never failed me, and You won't start now. I reject the lie of lack, the grip of fear, and the worry of insufficiency. Instead, I stand in faith, knowing that supernatural provision is my portion. Let hidden treasures be revealed and doors of favor swing wide. I declare divine acceleration and unexpected blessing are locating me even now.

As I obey You, I trust that You will cause every resource I need to manifest at the right time. I will not beg or strive, for I am a child of the King. You have already prepared those who will pour into me, and I receive with humility and gratitude.

In Jesus' name, Amen.

POSITION

ANOINTED FOR THIS ASSIGNMENT

> The Lord Yahweh's Spirit is on me; because Yahweh has anointed me to preach good news to the humble. He has sent me to bind up the broken hearted, to proclaim liberty to the captives, and release to those who are bound;
> —Isaiah 61:1 WEB

I boldly declare that the Spirit of the Lord is upon me. I am not here by accident—I am positioned on purpose and anointed for this very moment. Your power rests on me to bring freedom, healing, and breakthrough. I am equipped with divine authority to shift atmospheres and usher in the will of God.

Every chain is breaking because of the anointing. I carry good news for the brokenhearted, vision for the weary, and hope for the oppressed. I will not shrink back or stay silent. I am the vessel You've chosen, and I walk in divine confidence, knowing that Heaven backs me.

Let every room I enter be changed by Your presence in me. Let every assignment today be executed with boldness, grace, and clarity. I am not waiting for permission—I've been appointed, anointed, and released. I move forward, clothed in the oil of Your Spirit, ready to fulfill destiny.

In Jesus' name, Amen.

DAY 29

PRAISE

MY MOUTH IS FILLED WITH PRAISE

> My mouth shall be filled with your praise, with your honor all day long.
> —Psalms 71:8 WEB

I declare with boldness that my mouth is filled with Your praise today, O Lord! From the rising of the sun to its setting, I will bless Your holy name. You have been my dwelling place, my hiding place, and my song in the night. Your faithfulness has surrounded me in every season, and Your mercy has carried me through valleys and over mountains.

I will not be silent or subdued—I will proclaim Your greatness with joy. I lift my voice above the noise of life and crown You with honor, glory, and reverence. You alone are worthy of every breath I breathe and every word I speak. Let my worship shake the heavens and silence the accuser. Let my praise create an atmosphere for miracles and open doors.

Today, my life becomes an instrument of thanksgiving. Every action, thought, and word will magnify the goodness of my God. May Your presence saturate my environment and Your glory rest upon me. Praise is not just my response—it is my weapon, my language, and my lifestyle.

In Jesus' name, Amen.

Purpose

Preserved for Destiny

> Yahweh will keep your going out and your coming in, from this time forward, and forever more.
> —Psalms 121:8 WEB

I decree that today I am watched over by the Lord Himself. My going out and coming in are sealed by divine purpose. I do not walk aimlessly or casually—my steps are guided by eternity, and my movements are covered in purpose. There is nothing random about my life. I am preserved for destiny, and heaven is invested in my success.

Every hour of this day is ordained. I will not miss my moment, and I will not waste my strength. My decisions are Spirit-led. My heart is fixed on the One who keeps me in perfect peace. I will not be distracted by detours or delayed by discouragement. God is guarding my life, and nothing shall by any means harm me.

I declare that divine alignment is at work. I am where I need to be, doing what I've been called to do. My purpose is protected. My future is secure. And my today is fruitful because it is directed by the Lord of Hosts.

In Jesus' name, Amen.

PROTECTION

Empowered to Overcome

> For you have armed me with strength for the battle. You have subdued under me those who rose up against me.
> —2 Samuel 22:40 WEB

I arise today clothed in strength and anointed for victory. I declare that I have been empowered by God to overcome every adversary and every barrier. I will not shrink back, cower, or retreat. The strength of the Almighty has equipped my hands for battle and my feet to stand firm. No challenge shall overthrow me, for I have divine enablement to break through and to conquer.

I do not rely on natural power or carnal strategy. My strength comes from above. The Spirit of the Lord rises within me, and I am bold as a lion. Every attack launched against me is overturned. Every stronghold is shattered. I am advancing under the covering of divine authority.

Today, I walk as a warrior with peace in my heart and fire in my spirit. I am not just surviving—I am overcoming. I wield the weapons of heaven, and I stand in full victory, unshaken and undefeated.

In Jesus' name, Amen.

PROVISION

THE STOREHOUSE OF GOODNESS

> Oh how great is your goodness, which you have laid up for those who fear you, which you have worked for those who take refuge in you, before the sons of men!
> —Psalms 31:19 WEB

I declare that the goodness of God is laid up for me today. You, Lord, have stored treasures in secret places, and I access them by faith. I will not lack or labor in vain. You know how to provide beyond what I ask or imagine, and I trust in Your abundance with unwavering confidence.

Let Your generosity surround me like a shield. Release favor in places I didn't even know I needed it. Let resources chase me down, and let doors open without strain. I declare an overflow of provision—spiritually, financially, emotionally, and relationally. What I need has already been prepared.

I receive what heaven has reserved for me. I will not fear drought or depend on man, because my source is secure in You. I stand in awe of Your goodness and walk boldly into today knowing that all my needs are met by Your endless supply.

In Jesus' name, Amen.

Position

Fully Equipped by Grace

> Seeing that his divine power has granted to us all things that pertain to life and godliness, through the knowledge of him who called us by his own glory and virtue;
> —2 Peter 1:3 WEB

I declare that I lack nothing for life and godliness. Everything I need to walk in victory, to fulfill my calling, and to stand in righteousness has already been given to me through divine power. I am not waiting to be qualified—I am already equipped. I step into this day with confidence, clothed in grace, and aligned with purpose.

No area of my life is left uncovered. I have wisdom for the decisions ahead, strength for every task, and peace in every battle. I reject the lie of inadequacy and take my place as one who has been empowered by heaven. I embrace the identity, authority, and resources You've placed within me.

Today, I function from a place of overflow. I speak with clarity, move with boldness, and operate in excellence. I stand fully positioned—spiritually, mentally, and emotionally—to do great exploits. Nothing is missing, and nothing is broken. I am seated in heavenly places and walk with the confidence of one who has been chosen and prepared.

In Jesus' name, Amen.

DAY 30

PRAISE

MY HEART TRUSTS IN YOU

> Yahweh is my strength and my shield. My heart has trusted in him, and I am helped. Therefore my heart greatly rejoices. With my song I will thank him.
> —Psalms 28:7 WEB

I boldly declare that You, O Lord, are my strength and my song. You have lifted my soul and wrapped me in Your unwavering love. My heart is anchored in trust, and because I trust You, I rejoice. No matter what this day holds, I enter it with a spirit of praise, because I know You are the One who sustains me.

You are my shield when attacks rise against me, my light when the way seems dim, and my peace when chaos tries to invade. You have proven Yourself faithful time and again, and today, I respond with gratitude. I praise You not for circumstances alone, but because You are worthy—ever-present, ever-powerful, and ever-good.

My mouth will sing of Your goodness, and my heart will leap in joy. I release the sound of thanksgiving to shift the atmosphere over my life, over my home, and over every assignment You've given me. My praise is my weapon, and I use it today to exalt You above every obstacle.

In Jesus' name, Amen.

PURPOSE

YOU WILL SURELY DO IT

He who calls you is faithful, who will also do it.
—1 Thessalonians 5:24 WEB

I declare with confidence that the One who has called me is faithful, and He will bring to pass everything He has spoken over my life. Today, I walk in assurance that my purpose is not dependent on my strength, but on Your faithfulness. You are not a man that You should lie, and every word You've spoken over me is already finding its fulfillment.

I surrender afresh to Your call and trust Your process. Even in seasons of delay or transition, I know that Your timing is perfect. You are working behind the scenes, aligning hearts, shifting circumstances, and preparing the way for manifestation. I will not grow weary or doubt what You've declared—I believe You.

Let every assignment You've placed in my hands today be marked with excellence, grace, and divine precision. I receive clarity in decision-making, courage to step forward, and peace that surpasses all understanding. You are the Author and the Finisher of my purpose.

In Jesus' name, Amen.

PROTECTION

I Trust the Name of God

> Some trust in chariots, and some in horses, but we trust the name of Yahweh our God. They are bowed down and fallen, but we rise up, and stand upright.
> —Psalms 20:7-8 WEB

Today, I rise in the power of Your name, O God. I do not place my hope in natural strength, systems, or strategies—I place my trust fully in You. While others may depend on chariots and horses, I call upon the name of the Lord, my refuge and strong tower. Your name alone is my covering, and Your banner over me is victory.

Though the enemy may strategize to cause me to stumble, I stand firm because You uphold me. I declare that no weapon formed against me shall prosper, and every plan of the adversary is overturned now. I am not shaken by sudden fear or intimidation, for You have already gone before me to secure my path.

I walk today with divine confidence, knowing that heaven surrounds me. Angels are assigned to my life, and the power of the blood of Jesus shields my family, my territory, and my destiny. I am hidden under the shadow of Your wings, and I move forward in safety and strength.

In Jesus' name, Amen.

PROVISION

INCREASE IS MY PORTION

> May Yahweh increase you more and more, you and your children.
> —Psalms 115:14 WEB

I decree that today is a day of supernatural increase. The Lord, who delights in blessing His children, is causing me to multiply more and more. I receive divine favor, open doors, and the abundant flow of heaven into every area of my life. Increase is not a wish—it is my covenant right as a child of God.

I break agreement with lack, limitation, and scarcity. Every area that has been barren is now fruitful. I declare multiplication over my finances, my resources, my relationships, and my influence. The hand of the Lord is upon me to enlarge my territory and extend my reach for His glory.

I do not chase provision; I am overtaken by it. Opportunities are locating me, and divine connections are being aligned. I am blessed to be a blessing, and through me, others will experience the generosity and goodness of God.

In Jesus' name, Amen.

Position

You Light My Path

> For you will light my lamp, Yahweh. My God will light up my darkness.
> —Psalms 18:28 WEB

I boldly declare that the Lord has illuminated my darkness and positioned me to rise. Where confusion once clouded my vision, clarity now reigns. The light of Your presence reveals my next step and drives out every shadow of fear and hesitation. I am not stuck— I am strategically placed by Your hand.

You have pulled me out of low places and positioned me for increase, visibility, and influence. I no longer live under the weight of past mistakes or missed opportunities. You have given me fresh grace, and today I walk in boldness and divine alignment.

Order my steps, O Lord. Let me see clearly and move decisively. I embrace elevation, not by striving, but by surrender. As You continue to light my way, I will arise with confidence, walk in authority, and fulfill every assignment You've entrusted to me.

In Jesus' name, Amen.

Epilogue

You've done more than complete a 30-day prayer journey—you've established a spiritual rhythm that shifts atmospheres and strengthens your walk with God.

By rising early in worship, declaring truth, and aligning your heart with heaven each morning, you have planted seeds of purpose, power, and prophetic clarity. These are not just daily routines; they are the foundations of destiny.

Throughout this journey, you've learned to praise before problems, to listen before rushing, to declare God's promises before doubt takes root. And now you stand different—more anchored, more aware, more awake to the spiritual authority God has given you.

But this is only the beginning.

Commanding your morning is not a one-time challenge—it's a daily call. It's how you war in peace, walk in purpose, and win with consistency. The world will try to pull you back into chaos. But now you know: you don't have to react—you can rule. You don't have to drift—you can declare.

So rise up each day. Keep your sword in your hand and His Word in your mouth. Speak as one who knows heaven is listening and hell is trembling. You are not a victim of time—you are a steward of it.

Keep commanding. Keep declaring. Keep walking in victory.

Because every morning is a fresh chance to shape your destiny—with God leading the way.

The day is yours. Now rule it well.

Encourage Others with Your Story

If this prayer guide has strengthened your faith, deepened your intercession, or helped you stand in the gap for our nation, would you consider leaving a short review on Amazon? Your feedback not only encourages others but also helps more believers discover this resource and join in the prayer movement. Every review—just a few sentences—makes a difference and helps spread the call to command the morning. Thank you for being part of this movement.

More from PrayerScripts

COMMAND YOUR NIGHT: 30 Days of Prayers and Declarations to Secure Your Rest and Shape Your Tomorrow

Every night is a spiritual battlefield—what you do before you sleep can determine the course of your tomorrow.

Command Your Night: 30 Days of Prayers and Declarations to Secure Your Rest and Shape Your Tomorrow is a powerful devotional prayer manual designed to help you end each day in victory, not vulnerability. Whether you're battling anxiety, spiritual attacks, restlessness, or simply longing for deeper peace, this book equips you to reclaim your night with bold, Scripture-rooted prayers. Each night is structured around five strategic prayer themes: *Shut, Shield, Silence, Show, Sleep.*

COMMAND YOUR EVENING: 30 DAYS OF PRAYERS AND DECLARATIONS TO RELEASE THE DAY AND RECLAIM INTIMACY WITH GOD

> *There is a battle over every transition—and evening is one of the most spiritually neglected.*

Command Your Evening is the third book in the **Command Your Destiny** series—following *Command Your Morning* and *Command Your Night*. In heaven's rhythm, the evening is not just a wind-down—it's a window. A sacred hour where destinies are recalibrated, burdens are lifted, and hearts are re-centered in the presence of God. In *Command Your Evening*, you'll journey through 30 days of intentional, Spirit-led prayers and prophetic declarations centered around five key evening themes: **Release, Renew, Refocus, Rebuild,** and **Rest**.

STANDING IN THE GAP FOR COVENANT AWAKENING:

30 DAYS OF PRAYER FOR NATIONAL REPENTANCE, RIGHTEOUS LEADERSHIP & GOD'S SOVEREIGN RULE

What if your prayers could help turn the tide of a nation?

America stands at a spiritual crossroads. Division deepens, truth is under siege, and righteousness is being redefined. But God is still searching for those who will stand in the gap—intercessors who will cry out for mercy, justice, and national awakening.

Standing in the Gap for Covenant Awakening is a 30-day prayer guide for believers who sense the urgency of the hour and long to see their nation return to God.

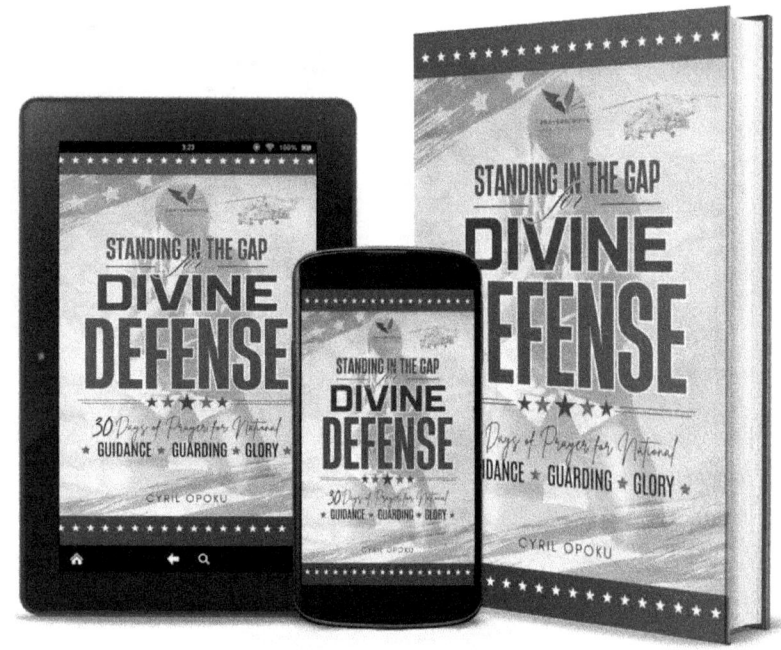

STANDING IN THE GAP FOR DIVINE DEFENSE:

30 DAYS OF PRAYER FOR NATIONAL GUIDANCE, GUARDING & GLORY

When the foundations of a nation feel as if they're shaking, prayer is the strongest fortress you can build.

Standing in the Gap for Divine Defense: 30 Days of Prayer for National Guidance, Guarding & Glory is your call to action—a 30-day journey of powerful, Scripture-rooted intercession that invites everyday believers to become watchmen on the walls for their nation. Drawing on timeless truths from God's Word, this devotional equips you to stand in the gap for your nation and **Seek Heaven's Wisdom, Secure Divine Protection,** and **Ignite Spiritual Awakening.** If you sense the urgency of the hour and long to see your country guided and guarded by the hand of God, open these pages. Stand in the gap. Watch Him move.

STANDING IN THE GAP FOR NATIONAL HEALING:

40 DAYS OF PRAYER FOR RECONCILIATION, RIGHTEOUSNESS, AND RESTORATION

What if your prayers could help heal a nation? What if God is waiting for someone—like you—to stand in the gap?

Standing in the Gap for National Healing: 40 Days of Prayer for Reconciliation, Righteousness, and Restoration is a bold, Spirit-filled call to action for believers who refuse to sit on the sidelines while their nation drifts further from God. In a time marked by division, confusion, and moral decline, this book equips you to pray with power, precision, and unshakable hope. Inside, you'll find 40 days of Scripture-based intercession divided into three strategic sections: **Peace, Unity & Reconciliation**, **Morality, Truth & Righteous Leadership**, and **National Restoration & Reformation**. It's time to stop watching history unfold—and start shaping it in prayer.

STANDING IN THE GAP FOR THE PRESIDENT:

50 DAYS OF PRAYER FOR LEADERSHIP, LOYALTY, AND LIFELINE

When a nation's leader is under spiritual siege, will you answer the call to stand in the gap?

Standing in the Gap for The President: 50 Days of Prayer for Leadership, Loyalty, and Lifeline is a bold, Scripture-saturated prayer guide for those who understand that the battles facing our leaders are more than political—they are spiritual. Assassination attempts, betrayal from within, and attacks on character and conscience are not just headlines—they're signs of the times. Inside, you'll find 50 days of strategic intercession divided into three high-impact sections: **Presidential Character & Leadership, Against Disloyal Insiders**, and **Against Assassination Attempts**. The future of a nation can shift through the prayers of the faithful. It's time to stand in the gap.

Scriptures & Prayers for Deliverance from Trouble:
40 Days of Prayer for When Life Feels Overwhelming

Are you walking through a season where life feels heavy, hope feels distant, and your prayers feel weak?

Scriptures & Prayers for Deliverance from Trouble is a 40-day journey of honest prayers and powerful Scriptures to help you find peace, strength, and healing when life is overwhelming. Each day offers a personal, Scripture-based prayer written in the language of real faith and raw trust. This devotional isn't about perfect words—it's about real connection with God when you need Him most.

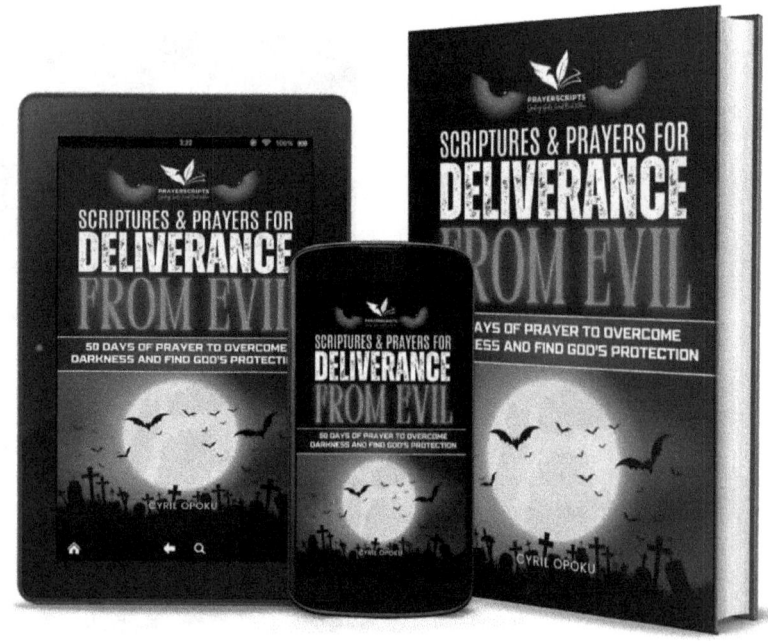

SCRIPTURES & PRAYERS FOR DELIVERANCE FROM EVIL:
50 DAYS OF PRAYER TO OVERCOME DARKNESS AND FIND GOD'S PROTECTION

When darkness presses in, how do you pray?

When fear grips your heart or unseen battles rage around you, you need more than generic words—you need Scripture, truth, and the steady hand of God to lead you through.

Scriptures & Prayers for Deliverance from Evil: 50 Days of Prayer to Overcome Darkness and Find God's Protection is a powerful devotional journey designed to help you pray boldly and biblically through seasons of spiritual warfare, oppression, fear, or uncertainty.

Scriptures & Prayers for Engaging the Enemy:

70 Days of Prayer to Rebuke the Enemy and Release God's Power

You weren't called to run from the battle—
you were anointed to win it.

Scriptures & Prayers for Engaging the Enemy: 70 Days of Prayer to Rebuke the Enemy and Release God's Power is a bold devotional for believers who are ready to rise, resist, and reclaim what the enemy has tried to steal. If you're tired of feeling spiritually outnumbered, this book will equip you to fight back—with Scripture in your mouth and power in your prayers. Over 70 days, you'll be guided through five strategic phases of spiritual warfare: (1) Rebuking the Enemy, (2) Releasing Terror Upon the Enemy (3) Praying for the Fall of the Enemy (4) Treading Upon the Enemy (5) When Heaven Strikes.

The war is real. But so is your victory.

SCRIPTURES & PRAYERS FOR COMBATING SPIRITUAL WICKEDNESS:

50 DAYS OF PRAYER TO OVERTHROW WICKED PLANS AND STAND IN GOD'S VICTORY

Are you facing opposition that feels deeper than the natural? Do you sense hidden resistance working against your progress, peace, or purpose? You're not imagining it—and you're not powerless.

Rooted in the authority of Scripture and fueled by bold, targeted prayers, *Scriptures & Prayers for Combating Spiritual Wickedness* equips you to confront darkness head-on. Each day features a focused Bible passage and a heartfelt, Scripture-based prayer designed to nullify ungodly counsel, disrupt demonic schemes, and establish God's victory in every area of your life.

www.ingramcontent.com/pod-product-compliance
Lightning Source LLC
Chambersburg PA
CBHW050637160426
43194CB00010B/1701